spiritual

GARMENTS

First published in 2006 by Decani Music Ltd, Oak House, 70 High Street, Brandon, Suffolk IP27 0AU

ISBN 10: 1 900314 17 7
ISBN 13: 978 1 900314 17 7

Printed by The Bath Press Limited, Lower Bristol Road, Bath BA2 3BL

Acknowledgements

Excerpts from the English translation of the *Introduction to the Lectionary for Mass* © 1981, International Committee on English in the Liturgy, Inc. (ICEL); excerpts from the English translation of the *Directory for Masses with Children* and *Sacrosanctum Concilium* from Documents on the Liturgy, 1963-1979: Conciliar, Papal, and Curial Texts © 1982, ICEL. All rights reserved.
Scripture texts and prayers from in chapter 11 are reprinted from The SUNDAY Liturgy of the Word Series with the permission of the publisher and copyright holders: Forum Katecheticum and Treehaus Communications, Inc., P.O. Box 249, Loveland, Ohio 45140 USA, (http://www.treehaus1.com/). All rights are reserved. Distributed in the United Kingdom by Viewpoint Resources Direct, 21 Point Hill, Greenwich LONDON SE10 8QW England.

For **Bernadette Brech**

Retired head teacher of St Mary's R.C.
Primary School, Clapham, London

spiritual

GARMENTS

A handbook for
preparing liturgical assemblies
in schools

Julie McCann

*I prefer to cut children's spiritual garments a little too
large for them to grow into, as they will in time. And
who knows what vivid image or hint of the beauty of
God will remain in their mind and memory?*
Dorothy Coddington

 Decani Books

Photo credits

Thanks to Brid Muldoon (teaching assistant) and Karen Pluckrose (headteacher) for sharing your gifts of vision so generously on a dull February day in half-term when you would rather have been at home cleaning.

Children in photos

Thanks to the following pupils of St Mary's who gave up a day of their holiday to come (in uniform!) to school and learn what hard work it is to be a celebrity at a photo shoot.

Joseph Abayomi	Nathan Marquez Dos Santos
Elaye Benson-Odum	Robert Mellon
Gabriella Blunden	Helen Naizghi
Tara Connor	Sheryl Palma
Dayna Dibua	Emma Pereira
Samson Frezgi	Teodros Tesfaye
Monica Gouveia	Jack Tituana
Natalie Kyei	Cameron Stokes

Illustrations

Children who have generously shared their thoughts and vision are: Natalie and Jack (above) and Isabel Azzopardi, Jobe Kenna and Antonia Kidd. The beginning of each chapter is illustrated by Karen Pluckrose. Thank you all. Drawing is not one of my gifts.

With thanks to:

✦ Christabel McLean and the London Borough of Lambeth Education Department for funding me to research and write this book under the Sabbatical Scheme for Experienced Teachers in Challenging Schools. This allowed me, and the cat, to keep warm and fed during the long winter days of writing

✦ the governors and headteacher of St Mary's School, Clapham for taking the risk of allowing me to take six weeks off to begin this project, knowing that I've been itching to do it for years and to Len Fletcher and Alison Adam who kept my pupils numerate , literate and musical while I was away

✦ to pupils, staff and parents of St Mary's School for having the courage to begin the journey from performance to prayer in our assemblies, for never letting me get away with being too pious and your enthusiastic interest in this writing venture

✦ to the Diocesan RE Advisors and the staff of schools I have visited for INSET training for your inspiration and strong desire to deepen the spiritual life of the children in your care and for stepping forward to stand around a parachute, sing and dance when I know you'd rather have not

✦ to Bernadette Farrell for teaching me that children are not just adults in the making, for writing songs that have brought life to our school and for getting the foreword to me when you were dealing with far more real issues of campaigning in south London

✦ to Martin Foster and Fr Allen Morris at the Bishops' Conference for numerous phone calls and visits to check liturgical facts, for lending me a pile of books (which I will give back, sometime) and for not putting a red pen through too many pages.

Contents

Foreword

As a child, school assembly was something I dreaded. It involved being squashed together like sardines, all trying to stay still. The room had a 'sad' smell. We were always under scrutiny. Most of the time I felt scared. The only relief was when someone threw up during a hymn.

But I was fortunate. I had a different experience at home, where there were simple moments of praise at meals, family time and bed-time. Somehow prayer became a habit.

Imagine if assembly was an experience children relished. Imagine if when they came together to worship they felt loved, safe and included. Imagine if this feeling was so strong that they became convinced they were part of the story. Imagine if they felt as special in this sacred space as the children who stepped through the wardrobe into Narnia. Imagine if they felt trusted enough to share their insights, their ideas, their individuality. Imagine if they then began to trust what they heard God saying to them in their hearts. Imagine if this became a habit for life.

Worship begins with an experience of wonder. This is something we should be trying to give our children. Liturgy is the 'doing' of praise. It is multi-dimensional. Its non-verbal elements are all the more potent with the very young.

In this book Julie has mapped out a journey of transformation; one on which she herself has led many children. Beginning with the basics, she guides us through actions to renew our liturgical experience.

In a climate of curriculums it can be difficult to remember the importance of dimensions less easily measured. This wonderful book helps us grasp the opportunity.

Bernadette Farrell

How to read this book

Don't you hate being told how to read something?

It's entirely up to you how you use this resource. Some may like to read it from cover to cover in one sitting – good luck! Others will dip into the sections they are first attracted to and then meander round the chapters. You may be looking for just one piece of information and will search for that in one paragraph alone.

Whatever your approach, I anticipate that you may discover passages that resonate with your situation and with which you totally agree, while there will be parts that puzzle, frustrate or even anger you. By the time this goes to print I'll probably have discovered such sections for myself too! You will certainly find repetition of fundamental issues, but this is done deliberately to ensure that no reader misses the important points. Try and read with a mind open to the spirit and to change, visualising your school and the people there.

1 Beginnings

I prefer to cut children's spiritual garments a little too large for them to grow into, as they will in time. And who knows what vivid image or hint of the beauty of God will remain in their mind and memory?

Dorothy Coddington, writing in 1923

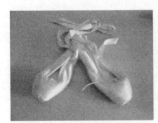

A story to begin

LAST YEAR I TOOK A GROUP OF YEAR 5 PUPILS TO THE Royal Ballet at Covent Garden. Each year we apply to go, but only about every fifth year do we get the coveted thirty tickets.

I knew that if I just sent home a letter about the trip very few reply slips would be returned, and I could be left with a mound of unsold tickets. Instead I would teach the children everything about the event. I would tell them the story (Giselle with the ethereal characters called the Willies – imagine how children enjoyed saying that over and over!), the recent history of the opera house itself, the rituals of ballet, the signs and symbols used by the dancers to convey meaning.

We watched a video clip one of the boys brought in (his sister was studying ballet at college) and drew stage sets, labelling 'front', 'backdrop', 'stage left' and 'stage right', the 'auditorium', and so on. Children love learning long, complex words.

The reply slips flooded in and every child in the group was able to make the trip.

I recall a moment that afternoon when I said to myself: 'Julie – you're getting paid for this!' Sitting in the sumptuous setting of the Royal Opera House, listening to a live orchestra and watching as the story of Giselle was danced out with such power and skill. Around me the children did not stir. They were so enthralled by the experience that they were sitting forward on their seats willing the dancers to keep dancing until the sun rose and they could be saved from the curse.

Sadly there were dozens of children from other schools, many of them much older than ours, who were bored, fidgety, talkative and unaware of what was being revealed in front of their eyes. Because our children had been introduced into the mysteries, they were able to enter into the world of ballet with confidence and a feeling that they had a right to be there.

9

Certainly they didn't understand everything that went on (for that matter, neither did I) but they left knowing that they could come to the ballet again and would grasp more and more each time. On the escalator on the way out, one of our boys was heard to comment: 'When I'm a man I'm going to bring my girlfriend here for a night out.' Good on him!

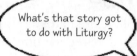

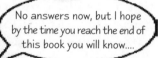

Introduction

I HAVE BEEN ASKED TO PUT TOGETHER THIS BOOK after leading a number of INSET days on liturgy in schools over the last few years.

I have been a teacher in a large primary school in south west London for eight years. Over that time we have worked to change our assemblies from class 'performances' to liturgies that reflect and form our identity as a Catholic Christian school. Our liturgical assemblies have become times to be looked forward to, regular times which come round each week, each term and each year and which feed us. Adults and children alike anticipate celebrating the same seasonal liturgies, familiar ones we have grown in understanding of over the years.

Who is this book for?

I imagine if you have read the blurb, opened the front cover and looked this far you have some connection with the worshipping life of a Christian school.

While writing, I have imagined this book being read by the class teacher in a primary school who has some responsibility for preparing and leading school assemblies with a large group of children. No doubt head teachers, teaching assistants, governors, parents, parish catechists, priests, chaplains and who knows, even a child, may pick up it too and be interested in what it has to say, but it is to my teaching colleagues whom I feel I am speaking. What we do in our schools needs special focus and this book hopes to serve the situations in which we teachers find ourselves.

As I have been working in the primary sector the liturgical practices described here are suited for that setting, but I believe they would work equally well in a secondary school since they are based on the existing liturgies of the church.

In a primary school most class teachers find themselves preparing an assembly several times a year. Cries of 'It's my turn for assembly next week!' or 'I can't think what to write for my assembly!' are heard in every staffroom in the land. Yet we often come to the task with little understanding or confidence. Most of us have not had the chance to study the liturgy or to spend time learning about the spiritual life of young people. These areas are rarely regarded as specialities, unlike music or sport where the 'expert' must be employed, and liturgy is not a focus at present in teacher training or induction courses.

Preparing an assembly, therefore, can fill teachers with dread. You may aim simply to sustain the children's interest and give them something 'good' to think about. Assembly time can degenerate into a showcase and competition between classes to do 'the best'. Yet celebrating with children requires thought, understanding and skill if it is going to be done well. (I wonder if non-Catholic members of staff actually spend more time learning about the liturgy of the church than those who were born into the tradition?)

The aims

Put very simply, the aims of this book are

➜ to help the class teacher in a Roman Catholic primary school in the UK know what liturgy is, and to feel familiar with its rituals

➜ to give the teachers the confidence to prepare and lead liturgies that are simple, prayerful and worthy

➜ to encourage children in their spiritual development and liturgical formation

➜ to provide examples of liturgies based on the rites of the church

No book can be 'all you will ever need'. Be wary of such claims. This book is certainly not the definitive text on liturgy in school. You may disagree with its suggestions or you may be inspired by them. However, it is rooted in real school experience, and the ideas it contains have been found useful and effective by many teachers who have heard them presented at INSET.

Going back to the sources

What I have aimed to do is go back to the original sources for guidance. I mean by this the official documents and given liturgies of the church. This is the way to approach the task, rather than searching for topical 'themes' to celebrate. In recent years dozens of 'instant assembly' books have appeared that give the 'busy school worship leader' a theme, a story, some questions to ask the children and a choice of songs. But if we look at what the Church to which we belong offers us in its scriptures, its seasons, its ritual actions, gestures and songs we find a richness beyond any packaged scheme.

Catholics are still influenced by a legacy of celebrating liturgy as though it was a performance to be watched. For many centuries until the mid-1960s the priest 'said' Mass and the congregation 'heard' it. People took rosaries and prayer books to church and sat in the pews to say their individual prayers while the Mass was taking place up on the sanctuary. The ritual could stand on its own without the presence of a congregation and as long as the rubrics were observed all would be well.

Since the Second Vatican Council (1962 – 65) the issue of how people take part in the liturgy has been given great attention.

In fact, the very first document issued by the Council was the Constitution on the Sacred Liturgy (1964), and at the heart of it are these words - revolutionary at the time.

> **The church earnestly desires** that all the faithful be led to that full, conscious and active participation in liturgical celebrations called for by the very nature of the liturgy. Such participation by the Christian people as 'a chosen race, a royal priesthood, a holy nation, God's own people' *(1 Peter 2:9; see 2:4-5)* is their right and duty by reason of their baptism. (§14)

The practical reforms of the liturgy following the Council not only included the introduction of vernacular languages (the move from Latin to English) but the radical reform of the liturgical texts and rituals. More than forty years on, however, we still haven't got the full benefit of these reforms. You could say that though the rituals have been renewed, the renewal of the people is still in progess. Forty years' experience since the Council shows that simply translating the Mass into English was not enough to engage the whole people's participation. Liturgy is not just a matter of reading words but of becoming involved in an action, from which lay people had been excluded for centuries. New skills needed to be learned by teachers and priests alike. But these skills and the knowledge which will enable us to be nourished by the experience of liturgy have still to be fully developed.

Any practice that we develop becomes ingrained, it becomes the norm. So it is important that the practice we aim for is good practice. I hope this book contributes to showing what that good practice is.

Church documents

School assemblies haven't directly been the subject of official comment , but we do have a number of very relevant documents to refer to and feed our understanding of liturgy. They have all been written to give direction for liturgical renewal.

From Rome:

The Constitution on the Sacred Liturgy (1964)
The Introduction to the Lectionary for Mass (1981)
The General Instruction on the Roman Missal (GIRM) (3rd edition, 2004)
**The Directory for Masses with Children (DMC) prepared by the Congregation for Divine Worship (1973)

From the Bishops' Conference of England and Wales:

**The Liturgy of the Word with Children Guidelines (1996) a commentary on the Directory for Masses with Children
Celebrating the Mass: a Pastoral Introduction (CTS, 2005)

** Begin with these two and read them often. They are practical, pastoral documents that offer ways of celebrating the Mass but also talk about initiating children into the ritual life of the Church.

Although official documents are often written in stilted and unfriendly language, these two are inspiring and easily read in one sitting. The focus is the Mass and how it may be adapted when children make up a large section of the congregation. But the principles remain the same for any act of worship.

Why don't I know these things?

Good question. Although many of you reading this will have been educated at Catholic schools and colleges, you may not have learned much about the renewal of the liturgical life of the very Church that was concerned with educating you. Often the rules (rubrics) seem too daunting and restrictive of your creative skills.

Perhaps, though, you were fortunate in having educators who knew the richness of the liturgical life of the church and were able to help you experience this as a young person. Maybe you are a Christian from another denomination who is able to apply what you know of celebrations in your own church to your present teaching role.

Somehow, though, we are all expected to know and to lead children in knowing as part of our professional role as a teacher.

Many teachers have been born since the Council. Before that time Catholics had many social and devotional practices to help form them. As the Mass became more participatory, these became less popular, until now the liturgy of Sunday is the main event by which we learn and form our identity. But the skills and knowledge which we need if we are to be fed and nourished by this experience have still to be fully developed.

Nurturing spirituality

Children are capable of deep spiritual experiences from a very early age.

Before they even find the words to express it they become aware of something other than themselves and their small worlds, something that is inspiring and good. An understanding of God is already within children and we are asked to give them the verbal vocabulary to express what they already experience. We can draw attention to an existing reality.

There is much talk nowadays of 'discovering the inner child'. I think that reaching back into that state of awe, trust, freedom and joy is what we are meant to do. Each of us has an individual spirituality within that is unique to us. For some it is connected to experiences of nature, for others it may take on more heavenly visions. This is not a call to be childish but to be childlike.

Through liturgy as well as through everyday experiences, children come to know that they are not alone in their spiritual beliefs and that there are ways of communicating with and about their spiritual nature. Too often in the past, people in the church have felt restricted in the exploration of this spiritual dimension that first emerged in infancy and still exists in us all, whatever age. The act of remembering – being intensively mindful – is part of our growth into maturity.

Schools that are attentive to the spirituality of their children and staff will know what a profound effect this care has not only on the life of the individual but on the behaviour and attitudes of all in their relationships with one another. Our spiritual life cannot remain private but urges us to respond in action. We don't just call upon 'god' when things are going wrong in our lives.

Home, school and parish

> **The purpose of adapting liturgy for children** is to lead them into full, conscious and active participation in the liturgy of the parish. *Guidelines*, p.5

> **The Christian communities** to which the individual families belong or in which the children live also [i.e. as well as parents] have a responsibility toward children baptised in the Church. By giving witness to the Gospel, living fraternal charity, actively celebrating the mysteries of Christ, the Christian community is the best school of Christian and liturgical formation for the children who live in it. *DMC §11*

Those of us working in Catholic schools would love to believe that all the children come from families that choose to make church part of their Sunday routine and are able to teach their children the prayers and values of our faith.

True, 'attending Mass' is certainly not all it takes to live a holy life. Without action and response we are very poor indeed. The parents of our children have made a definite choice in sending their children to a Catholic school, indeed many have gone to great lengths to get their child admitted. I believe that many parents yearn for something in the way of formation for themselves too, and children at a faith school often lead parents back to the church. I can see that in promulgating the Directory for Masses with Children the Church recognised a need for liturgical formation:

> **Today the circumstances in which children grow up** are not favourable to their spiritual progress. In addition, sometimes parents barely fulfil the obligations of Christian education which they undertake at the baptism of their children. *DMC §1*

However, the truth is that in many schools the majority of children are not celebrating with a parish community on a Sunday. Therefore what we do in liturgy in school is vital in forming the life-long habits of young people that can take them into adulthood.

By introducing children to the rituals, prayers, language, symbols, colours, songs and seasons of the church we are connecting them to a body far wider than the school boundary: in fact, the Body of Christ. If the way we celebrate in school is so different from what is experienced by the parish community on a Sunday then children will begin to believe that 'liturgy is for kids' and may well reject all they have been given by the time they're confirmed. Singing twee children's songs and talking down to children does them, and us, no favours. To use two words often found in writing about liturgy, it is neither dignified nor worthy.

> **Above all, the priest should be concerned about the dignity,** clarity, and simplicity of his actions and gestures. In speaking to the children he should express himself so that he will be easily understood, while avoiding any childish style of speech. *DMC §23*

15

We need to work towards a continuity between Sunday celebrations and the prayer life of the school. Sing some of the same songs sung in church, decorate the hall with the right seasonal colours, read from the same Biblical translation, learn the gestures and rituals of the Church. The school, however, cannot be a substitute for the parish, where celebrating the Sunday eucharist week by week is the norm.

In forming children in liturgy, the first source of instruction for all age groups should be the parish priest.

Mass in school

At the Synod of bishops held in Rome in 1967, the president of the Consilium for the Implementation of the Constitution on the Liturgy said explicitly that evolving a way of celebrating Mass with children could not be a matter of 'creating some entirely special rite but rather of retaining, shortening, or omitting some elements or of making a better selection of texts.' (DMC §3).

The Mass, also called the Eucharist, is the principal liturgy of the church, the centre of its life. (The word 'Mass' comes from the Latin phrase *Ite missa est* spoken at the dismissal). Having an understanding of the Mass as word and ritual action is vital for understanding any other liturgy.

But various other kinds of celebration may also play a major role in the liturgical formation of children and in their preparation for the Church's liturgical life. (DMC §13).

> Sometimes it is preferable to have common prayer to which the children may contribute spontaneously, either a common meditation or a celebration of the word of God. These celebrations continue the eucharist and lead to deeper participation in later eucharistic celebrations. *(DMC §2)*

I wonder if we have got into the habit of celebrating Mass too often. It could be celebrated for every school occasion – start and end of the year, blessing of the building, welcoming new parents, remembering the dead, etc. Many teachers look for a theme for each Mass to suit the occasion, and can be disappointed in not finding the exact wording in the prayers and readings offered that they are looking for.

Consider if it might be more appropriate to celebrate a Liturgy of the Word and a ritual action that is not eucharistic. In the school year, there are a number of days on which, with the whole church, we are obliged to participate in a eucharistic liturgy (see p.82) but other feasts and seasons can be celebrated with a liturgy centred on the Word.

In this book I have chosen to write about the Liturgy of the Word as a distinct form of liturgy instead of writing about the Mass, although all the same principles and elements apply. So the passages quoted in this book may refer to 'Mass' but the principles apply equally fully when celebrating a Liturgy of the Word with children.

2   What are we doing?

B EFORE LOOKING SPECIFICALLY AT LITURGY in the life of a Catholic primary school, we should clarify the meaning of the terms used.

Official legislation from the government uses the terms 'collective worship' and 'spiritual development'. The local diocese may add 'liturgy' and 'prayer life' to that list but the everyday vocabulary of the Catholic primary school is more likely to be 'prayer', 'assembly' and 'Mass'.

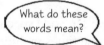

There are, of course, the dictionary definitions and you will find further variation of meaning depending on who you talk with. The SACRE (Standing Advisory Body for Religious Education) for each local education authority has defined collective worship in a wide variety of ways, as have the RC dioceses. Depending on who comes to inspect the school under Section 48, you may be asked to comment on the 'prayer life', 'worship' and/or 'spiritual development' of the school community. Some ecumenical documents choose to use the conjunct term 'worship/liturgy'.

What vocabulary does your school's Religious Education or Worship policy use? It is important to reach mutual agreement between staff and governors on what terms are used in your school and diocese.

The religious life of the school

Let's start a step further back by looking at the whole religious life of the school.

Many schools have 'Gospel values' or 'centred on Christ' in their mission statement, since it is belief in this Gospel that nourishes us and colours all that we do as a school.

Our aim is to recognise Christ in ourselves and in others, and so to be the body of Christ in the world. We belong to a particular Christian tradition and follow the practices of this church in our quest for and expression of the Gospel, the good news of Jesus Christ. We believe that we should celebrate God's presence in our lives and respond to God's invitation to relationship in word and action.

As adults employed in this school, we hope to share the values of the Gospel and the teachings of the church in all curriculum areas as well as at play times, when dealing with arguments, in our meetings with parents, when talking with a crying child - indeed in the whole life of the school.

It permeates all that we are and do:

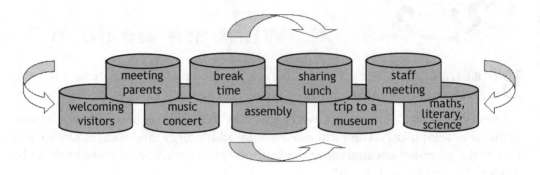

Particular moments set aside

Then there are particular moments in the week when we set aside specific time to explore and reflect on the religious nature of our lives. These times include religious education lessons, prayer times in the classroom or hall, assemblies of a religious nature, hymn singing, meditation and other events that may be specific to your school:

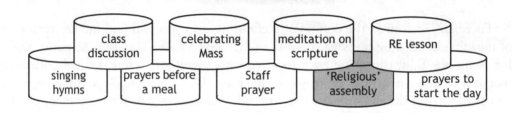

The assembly - defining the term

This book is primarily concerned with the event called 'assembly', although the principles apply to the Mass as well.

First we need to define what this word means.

'Assembly' in church language can refer to the body of people gathered together for worship.

It is also a generic term, which is peculiar to the UK (look in religious education books published in the US or Canada and you rarely find an 'assembly') for a particular school event.

A school assembly can be any gathering of large numbers of children for a variety of purposes. The purpose can often be determined by the prefixed word: class assembly, prayer assembly, good work assembly, awards assembly, singing assembly and so on.

Sometimes two purposes are combined in the one assembly, for example weekly awards given after the school has met for prayer. A 'religious' assembly is one where the school's religious life ('ethos') is acknowledged in a large group setting:

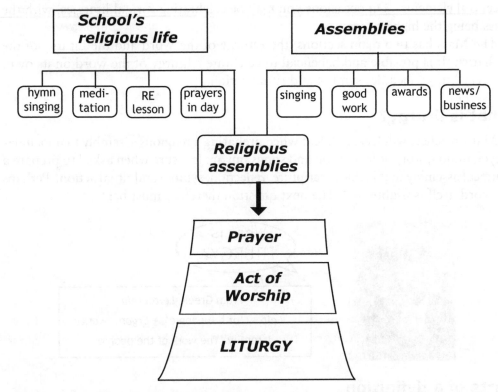

Prayer, Reflection, Worship

These are elements that may appear in an assembly. Each of them can stand alone. All of them combine, with ritual action, to make liturgy. To some extent they are all different names for the same thing, but for the purposes of this book I use 'liturgy' to mean the most formal, structured kind of religious activity.

Prayer

Prayer is communication with God. It involves listening as well as speaking in thanks, praise, petition and blessing. Prayer can be an individual or communal activity. Prayer can use words that others have composed or words of our own. Prayer need not involve any words at all.

Reflection & meditation

Developing our spiritual nature through reflecting on the presence of God in the world and in scripture. Silently pondering our lives.

Worship

Worship is the giving of honour and praise to God who is most worthy of it. Worship is a response to our experience of life. (Some churches use the word 'Worship' instead of 'liturgy'.)

Symbol

Liturgy

Liturgy always includes prayer, reflection and worship. It involves participation through symbol and action. The Eucharistic Liturgy (the Mass) is the summit of all liturgy. We may also celebrate other forms of liturgy such as a Liturgy of the Word.

Ritual action

19

It is likely that most of your assemblies are acts of worship with prayer and reflection as central elements. On occasions you may be celebrating formal liturgies, with the Mass being the highest form.

The Mass has two main sections: the Liturgy of the Word and the Liturgy of the Eucharist. It is possible and beneficial to celebrate a liturgy of the word on its own.

Every liturgy includes symbol and ritual action.

What is liturgy?

Many teachers will feel confident when preparing a religious assembly that includes prayer, drama, story, information and songs but are less sure when asked to prepare a liturgical assembly that includes scripture, reflection, symbol and ritual action. Perhaps the word itself is frightening. The next question therefore must be:

What is LITURGY?

From Greek *Leitourgia*
Leitos, 'of the people' + *Ergon*, 'work
Literally 'The work of the people'

Parts of a definition

Here are some general principles of liturgy taken from the Liturgy of the Word with Children Guidelines published by the Bishops' Conference of England and Wales Liturgy Office in 1996:

❖ **Liturgy is the praise and worship of God**

God is present in our lives in this world. We acknowledge God's continuous presence in creation and praise God simply for being. We thank God for the gifts we are given.

❖ **Liturgy is the source and summit of the Church's life and ours**

Everything about our lives is brought to liturgy. At the same time liturgy gives us the strength to go out and live our lives. Sunday is the pivotal point of the week when we come to the eucharistic liturgy (the Mass) to reflect on the past week and be challenged and strengthened for the week to come. We are fed by Christ present in his Word and his Body.

❖ **The purpose of the liturgy is to build up the members of Christ's body, to strengthen us in preaching Christ**

Humans are social beings who come together at times of sorrow, happiness, need and change. We gather, talk, tell stories, take part in some common activity and then leave one another's company, changed by the experience.

Liturgy follows this pattern. It is a communal activity. It can only be done with other people. In fact, if you hold on to that fact when preparing school liturgies then they will become alive to feed the community you serve. Although prayer can be private, liturgy is not. There are books full of prayers and devotions for private meditation and reflection, but these are not liturgies.

- and parts of a description

❖ **Liturgy is action and symbol; it speaks to the whole person, it involves all the senses: sight, touch, sound, taste and smell**

Liturgy is not only the formal texts and rituals that are written down to be followed. Liturgy uses all our senses to involve our whole bodies, not just our minds. In its fullness, liturgy touches the whole of our beings through the ordinary things of life:

Our **eyes** meet Christ in seeing the symbols such as the candles, the bible, the cross, water, oil, ashes, bread and wine. There are also the seasonal colours, works of art, banners and plants to feast our eyes on.

Our **bodies** meet Christ in touching one another, in holding and using symbols, in praying and singing, and in moving through the gestures of kneeling, walking in procession, dancing and standing.

Our **ears** meet Christ in hearing scripture proclaimed, in listening to music and song, in silence and prayer.

Our sense of **smell** meets Christ in the fragrant incense and flowers, the scented oils, the rich wine and the warm bread.

Our sense of **taste** meets Christ in the bread and wine.

❖ **In liturgy we discover the riches of prayer, through word and gesture, silence and stillness**

Note that 'silence' and 'stillness' here are two distinct elements.

We can be *still* with our bodies while speaking or singing. We can be *silent* with our lips while walking in a procession or marking the sign of the cross on a friend's hand. It is important in liturgy to allow time for deep silence, which you should lead into gently, perhaps with music.

Children can easily learn to be still, not in a forced or rigid way, but prayerfully and in a relaxed manner. They see how to do this best by observing the adults around them. Prayer is 'caught, not taught'.

Who needs liturgy?

We do! We are called to worship so that God can give us the gifts prepared for us. God is waiting for us to answer the call, to share with us the 'life in all its fullness' which Jesus promised and which we yearn for.

Strictly speaking God does not *need* our praise and thanksgiving. God is like a selfless parent or friend who waits for us to get in touch but does not force us to, yet rejoices when we answer. A prayer from the Missal expresses what it means:

> You have no need of our praise,
> **yet our desire to thank you is itself your gift.**
> Our prayer of thanksgiving
> adds nothing to your greatness,
> but makes us grow in your grace
>
> *Preface of Weekdays, IV*

Not just human or divine -

Liturgy is a meeting point of the human and the divine. It should not become too focused either on human concerns and needs, or on cerebral images of the divine.

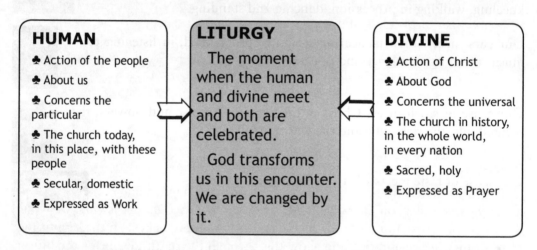

HUMAN	LITURGY	DIVINE
♣ Action of the people	The moment when the human and divine meet and both are celebrated.	♣ Action of Christ
♣ About us		♣ About God
♣ Concerns the particular		♣ Concerns the universal
♣ The church today, in this place, with these people	God transforms us in this encounter. We are changed by it.	♣ The church in history, in the whole world, in every nation
♣ Secular, domestic		♣ Sacred, holy
♣ Expressed as Work		♣ Expressed as Prayer

- but both

Liturgy is a communication with an everlasting God and the whole church throughout history. If liturgy is only about *us* then we lose this connection. Liturgy does involve our individual concerns, emotions and needs, because we bring all of ourselves to the celebration, but we should see ourselves as part of something much bigger, the Kingdom.

Conversely, if liturgy is only about God and uses needlessly complex language and rituals then we begin to believe God is not concerned with the here and now.

The way we celebrate liturgy forms our image of God. That's why we shouldn't just celebrate what we like when we like, because we might simply be creating the kind of God we want. Instead, we should let ourselves be guided by the Gospel and the liturgy of the Church.

Christ is present in the continuous liturgy of the church. By celebrating the liturgies of the church year and proclaiming the Gospel readings of the season we are meeting Christ, responding to that message and going out into the world as community.

Liturgy is not entertainment

..our children will be entertained or occupied, but their attention will have been drawn only to the surface of things, not to the inner, more universal realities those surfaces suggest.

The Welcome Table, p.28

Sometimes entertainment *is* the reason for assembling in the hall – a theatre company visit, the school choir performance, Year 6 pupils putting on their leaving play. But when we gather for liturgy we should not come expecting to be entertained.

Neither is liturgy a lesson or a competition between classes.

Won't the children be bored doing liturgy?

Bored?

Not if we take care to prepare them for what will happen and guide them to reflect on their experience afterwards. After all, this is what we would do for school trips and visits. If the adults in the school believe in the significance of what they are celebrating and show this through their attitude during the liturgy, then the children will see how important it is.

The pull to introduce novelty is very strong and it is tempting to say 'I want my assembly to be the best this term.' But liturgy should not be distracted by novelty or be seen as a performance. It should be full of the familiar in its songs, stories, symbols and actions. We should feel we are coming to something we already know.

This means that the liturgy may remain very much the same from week to week, year to year. But *our encounter* with it is different, because we ourselves are different each time.

The leader's role is to enable that encounter to happen without distraction.

Not a 'children's activity'

Liturgy, in school as in church, is not a 'children's activity'. It is an act of the whole community (the assembly), young and old. Children and adults alike need to be led into an understanding of the liturgy so that they can have it speak to them, so that it can reveal something of God and their spiritual lives to them.

It is true that without preparation ('catechesis') beforehand children may well be bored or fidgety and that's when the entertainers want to move in to liven up everything and make it 'interesting for the children'.

But what could be more stimulating to a child's spiritual being and development than watching candles being lit, listening while clear water is poured into a large bowl, making the sign of the cross across the body, touching a wooden cross, smelling the rising incense? Go for what is ordinary, simple, dignified and part of our tradition. No puppets or clowns are necessary!

Remember –

🖝 In the proclamation of the Gospel (the 'breaking of the word'), Christ is as present to us as in the Eucharist (the 'breaking of bread'.)

🖝 Liturgy is personal but not individual. It is about discovering God together in the ordinary things of life – story and symbol.

🖝 Liturgy is not an end in itself – it always leads outwards to everyday life.

🖝 Liturgy connects us with other Christians throughout time and place

Part of the great story

I had a profound experience of being part of the universal and historical church while on a visit to Salisbury Cathedral in winter while writing this book.

The weather outside was extremely cold and windy, so I had spent much of the afternoon on my own (I was due to visit a school the next day) scuttling between the draughty cloisters, the welcoming tearoom and the chapter house with its wonderful medieval carvings detailing the events of the old testament. Chilled to the bone I entered the cathedral in the gloom of early evening and wandered the aisles and chapels while the girls' choir rehearsed for evensong. There was much laughter and lightness in their presence and I reflected on how wonderful it was to be hearing female voices in this ancient place of prayer.

Since I was staying at a bed and breakfast and was destined for a lonely meal for one that evening I chose to stay on for the service, partly to kill time. With the young singers, clergy and congregation there could only have been about fifty of us altogether huddled into the choir stalls at the chancel end of the cathedral. Only this area was lit, the rest of the building was in shadowed darkness. The prayers and psalms were chanted beautifully and with great certainty and an easy flow. All was peaceful.

With no warning or buildup there was suddenly an enormous clap of thunder and huge flashes of lightning beamed through the darkened cathedral. We could see right back to the nave door. The girls' faces made no attempt to hide the terror felt inside but their voices continued with only the slightest wavering. Over and over in the next fifteen minutes we shuddered with the thunder and gasped with each flash of light.

Towards the end of the service, calm returned to the building and I left feeling somehow connected with the many generations who through centuries have sat in that same cathedral listening to the same psalms and prayers and experiencing the same dramatic weather. I was not alone. There are those who have gone before and those who will come after.

Perhaps the highlight of the experience was leaving by a side door to find the cathedral green no longer green but an amber lamp-lit white. The thunderstorm had brought a deep blanket of snow that obscured the pathways leading back into the city. I wasn't the only lost soul – I fell into conversation with a fellow traveller, also in Salisbury just for the night. The expected lonely meal for one became a life-giving meal for two.

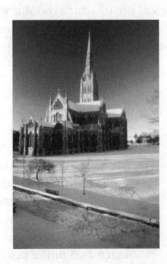

3 Liturgy: not a lesson

> The Christian family has the greatest role in teaching [these] Christian and human values.. Thus Christian education, provided by parents and other educators, should be strongly encouraged in relation to liturgical formation of children as well. DMC §10

> The liturgy of the future, which these children will help to create, depends upon the liturgical formation which the children receive now.
> *The Welcome Table, p.23*

> It is not right to separate [such] liturgical and eucharistic formation from the general human and Christian education of children. Indeed it would be harmful if liturgical formation lacked such a foundation. DMC §8

We have seen that liturgy is not entertainment nor is it an RE lesson, and so this chapter is concerned with 'liturgical formation' and how it is a discrete process.

In reflecting on the liturgical life of your school it will become important to clarify the distinctions between RE lessons, liturgical formation and doing liturgy. Of course, there will be some overlaps between these events but each has its different qualities and purposes.

In outline:

the difference between an RE lesson, 'liturgical formation' and doing liturgy

• **The RE lesson** This usually takes place in the classroom and is the 'teaching about' religion.

Many schools use a pre-written programme such as 'Here I Am' (HIA) to form the basis of these lessons. There may be opportunities in the chosen programme to hear about the teachings of the church, to listen to passages from scripture, to learn a common prayer, to share personal stories and to make connections between our faith and others'. The programme of lessons may include times of prayer and reflection.

• **Liturgical formation** Part of an RE lesson can be learning about the language and rituals of the church. It is certainly part of the HIA material. This process allows us to come to the liturgies with some initial understanding and connection. The formation also requires a brief reflection on liturgy after the event with the opportunity to describe the experience, ask questions and consider how it affects our lives.

• Liturgy   This is the time of 'doing' which takes place in the classroom, hall or church. It may be part of the whole RE programme but is not a teaching/learning time. You may need to think about having separate RE and liturgy co-ordinators to lead these two areas in school.

Try to be clear about what you're doing and make sure there is time for all three of the above. The main pitfall is using liturgy time as teaching time. Although liturgy may, through its actions and symbols, teach us and form us, these are not its primary aims. However, in order to access liturgical language and actions it is important to teach about liturgy in RE lessons.

Liturgical formation: three stages

The format of liturgical formation is threefold: before, during and after liturgy. Just as each liturgy follows a structure so the parts surrounding it have shape too. Both are processes that rely on repetition; they are cycles that help us to enter the encounter.

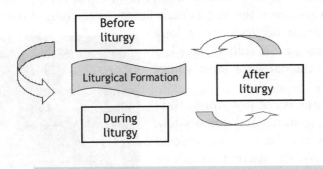

1. Before liturgy– 'catechesis'

preparation is essential to good liturgy

Preparation is essential to good liturgy. Individual liturgies should grow from reflection on the scriptures of the day, how it relates to the faith experience of the people involved, and how best the Gospel can be shared with children. *Guidelines* p 16

Liturgy must hold up for us both a mirror to see who we are and a vision to see who we can be. *Tufano p8*

As in the story of the trip to the Royal Ballet at the beginning of the book, it is important to prepare children for any experience they are about to take part in.

Many of the liturgical elements described in this book require some practical preparation by each class before the whole school or large group gathers together on the day of the liturgy.

Although we may be following the language and rituals of the church in our school celebrations, it is important to interpret them for this particular group of people, at this time and in this place.

Little and often

This need not be a lengthy process. Rather, it may be best for it to be a short one, but one that is repeated each year as the same liturgy is encountered again and again.

It is a very useful preparation to have the main reading of the forthcoming assembly for class teachers to read and discuss with their children, and an outline of the liturgy giving prayers and responses that may need to be explored and learned.

There may need to be a time set aside to walk through the procession with those involved, to train the readers, to rehearse solo singers, to show prayer readers where to stand.

But don't practise the whole liturgy like a dress rehearsal before a concert, and don't bring the whole school together to go through the entire liturgy.

It is not necessary or possible to explain the meaning of each word used to the children. That understanding may come through the 'after the liturgy' discussion or, more likely, many years down the line as each liturgy is celebrated over and over.

Preparation takes time; it occurs over a long period and it can be done more fully if there is a long interval between the dates for large school celebrations.

And remember liturgy is not just words. Talk through the symbols, gestures and colours too. During the liturgy is not the time for lengthy explanations about, say, the Advent wreath or the Easter candle. When you do get to the liturgy, though, let symbols speak for themselves. They are best understood by doing them in the context of the liturgy.

Questions for 'before liturgy':

- Do the children know how to use the silences?
- Can they join in with some or all of the singing?
- Do they know the response to the prayers?
- Do they know that a 'reading' is a story to be listened to?
- What are they able to participate in now?
- What skills of participation may they still need to develop?

2. During the liturgy

By the very fact of celebration children easily come to appreciate some liturgical elements, for example, greetings, silence, and common praise. Such celebrations, however, should avoid having too didactic a character.
DMC §13

> **Liturgy forms us, it moulds the way we feel about ourselves, others, the church, the world and God.**

Liturgy forms us, it moulds the way we feel about ourselves, others, the church, the world and God. It prompts us into action.

The attitude we have towards liturgy and the way we choose to celebrate will form us, and those in our care, as Christians.

So if we want to be active, inspired and hopeful in our lives as Christians then our liturgies most be so too.

During the liturgy is not the time for lengthy explanations about symbols, as said above. That should have been done beforehand in class (or as we often do in a hymn practice when learning songs for a liturgy). The celebration is the time to do what we know.

The way you do liturgy will show how you feel about it. To carry the Gospel book high while singing Alleluia expresses how you value the contents of that book. If you handle the symbols with reverence you are saying how precious their meaning is. You do not need a running commentary to explain everything, just as a parent does not need to keep saying 'I love you'.

Remember liturgy is not just about us or just about God but about the two joining together. The scripture reflections should not be one person's ideas only but be open to the shared presence of Christ in all, young and old. Liturgy is not just about the past or just about the present, but about all time. Secular and sacred, work and prayer, body and spirit - liturgy is an interaction between the human and the divine that leads to an active response.

3. After the liturgy - 'mystagogy'

Over and above what has been said already, all liturgical and eucharistic formation should be directed toward a greater and greater response to the Gospel in the daily life of the children. *DMC §15*

Mystagogy is the moment when life and ritual crash into each other and all kinds of amazing insights result. *Tufano*

The third part of the cycle is the reflection after a liturgy which can be referred to as the 'mystagogy', (literally, instruction in the mysteries.)

This term refers to the fifty day period of Eastertime, when people who have just been baptised meet to talk about what they have seen and heard at the Triduum liturgies, just as the travellers to Emmaus did when they shared their experiences of meeting Jesus on their journey after he had gone: 'Did not our hearts burn within us?'

So what mystagogy does is to 'break open'. This time of thinking back and retelling is a natural response to a communal experience, a life skill that needs to be developed in all of us. In a brief time of reflection we go deeper into our encounter and get insights of understanding from others who were there too.

In many ways this already happens in spontaneous conversations between adults, but children can be guided into doing it too. A brief time spent with children after a liturgy, perhaps at the end of the day, will allow questions and responses to emerge in a supportive and encouraging way.

A format for breaking open the liturgy:

- What can you remember of what happened?
- Describe what you saw, heard, said, did, smelt and tasted
- What does the liturgy mean for your own life? How will it change you?
- Do you have any questions?
- What will you hold on to and remember from the liturgy?

In our school, break time follows most assemblies so the staff head up to the staffroom and often comment on what they have just experienced. 'I never knew that about ...', 'Why do we ...?' 'I really enjoyed...' 'That reminded me of...' Our parish priest often joins the school community for assemblies, not as leader but as a member of the school community. There have been many times when the staffroom discussion has led to questions for and discussion with him and each other.

It is after liturgy when we realise that what we have been taught in RE lessons or what we know of church teachings is true because we have experienced it in liturgy. We have been given a glimpse of the Kingdom, an insight into heaven.

But we cannot rest or remain unchanged after such an experience. Liturgy demands that we respond in action. We leave the gathering longing to serve, to communicate, to act differently. We are fired up to do our part in (re)creating the kingdom of justice. We desire to bring about the oneness that God too desires. It's no small thing that we are doing!

Repetition

we are ritual people and learn through repetition

Participating in liturgy forms our habits because we are ritual people and learn through repetition and copying. *Guidelines*

Of course, we don't celebrate each liturgy just once, then leave it behind to 'invent' a new one for the next year.

One of the joys of working with children is their need and demand for repetition. The church also recognises the power of repetition for all ages and does not reinvent new rituals each year. In fact, there are detailed rules and guidelines for keeping the rites the same. This way we are continually connected with the universal church and can mark our own growth each year by standing inside the same liturgies.

We all have our routines for getting up in the morning. Some can't function without that first cup of tea, others have to eat breakfast before taking a shower, you might set the alarm half an hour before you need to get up so that you can snooze awhile. As children, we felt the safety and comfort of routines in our day too.

When the routine is altered we can feel uncertain and less able to take on the challenges around us. Try to alter a single word in a child's familiar bedtime story and you'll hear protest from the listener. The exact words are what the child needs to hear and any attempt to skip a few pages or paraphrase a dauntingly long speech will be spotted.

The liturgy too is full of routine: rituals of word and action that are to be done again and again. We begin to feel comfortable in the sameness, and to know that we have a right and duty to belong in the liturgy. Songs, responses, gestures and prayer begin to come from the heart because they are so deeply ingrained.

Of course, these rituals, as with many habits in relationships, may become lifeless and empty. It is the changing events of life that give the familiar new meaning. It is with the changing seasons and the cycle of readings that the rituals take on new significance.

As we come again to the same words and rituals, we can ponder and discover another layer of understanding that perhaps a year ago we could not have reached in to. If a school's liturgies are constantly changing, recreated every time from a blank canvas 'in case the children get bored' then we are missing the point and remaining on the surface. Nobody can take in everything in one liturgy. Different people notice different things. It is often the case that we hear what we need to hear, and we believe this is spirit of God working in us to lovingly provide us with what we most yearn for.

Have the courage to celebrate the same liturgies each year

So, have the courage to celebrate the same liturgies in school over and over at the same times each year. Reflect on what happened last time. Could a better song be chosen? Did the seating help us to pray? Do we know prayers this year that may be more appropriate? Change one or two elements as your experience guides you, but don't start from scratch every time. Remember - the liturgy remains the same ; we grow into it over the years. Our understanding is not static but will become richer each year we come to this day to do the same thing one more time.

Many of us have the experience of Christmas Midnight Mass. As a child, concentration was perhaps given to keeping awake, avoiding inhaling too much incense, wondering if Father Christmas will have arrived by the time you get home, singing a carol you recognise from school, waving across the aisle to a little friend. If that is still your experience as an adult then something is wrong! Nowadays thoughts may turn to listening to the readings; finding a phrase I could swear I've never heard before: 'You have made their gladness greater, you have made their joy increase'; pondering myself the utterly amazing truth that the child was GOD with flesh and loud cries; remembering family who are not here as they have died this year, and so on. .

This same applies to the Easter Vigil. I wish we could be asked to give in our watches at the beginning so that we could relax into the lengthy night with no sense of time. Each year, the words of the psalms become more and more familiar and this year I found I could sing whole verses by heart. As I witnessed the five adults from my parish drenched in water as they were baptised I remembered back to the many years I have stood to watch this ritual.

4 Doing liturgy with children

W E HAVE READ SO FAR THAT LITURGY is 'the work of the people' and that there is a process of formation surrounding the liturgy. Now we move to thinking about liturgy in the specific context of primary schools.

You will have come across books with titles such as 'Celebrations for children' or 'Big assemblies for little people'. The word 'for' implies that the liturgy is something put on for the benefit of children – an event planned, prepared and 'performed' for their enjoyment and development. Think instead of using 'with' and you will be on the right track.

Remember: liturgy is something we all do together, adults and children alike.

'Playing' at liturgy

We know from our training and from our experience as teachers that children have a need to play in order to make sense of the world around them. Play allows them to rehearse relationships, establish roles and feel at home in new situations. Sadly, play does not appear in the curriculum beyond Foundation Stage (age 3 to 5 years) and many will feel that children are missing out because of this.

Have you noticed how children will often copy the gestures at Mass? Or how they mouth along with the words of the prayers even if they don't know the words? Have you been with excited children at the sign of peace when they get to shake hands with those around them? Think about how children might feel more at home in the rituals and language of the church if they are given the opportunities at school or at home to 'play at liturgy' as they would other familiar scenes. This isn't such an alien idea if you consider that what we are doing in liturgy is 'playing' at the Kingdom. We are rehearsing our parts for heaven when we will be praising God continuously.

The Reception Class home corner or year 1 shop could easily be transferred into 'church' with colourful cloths, cardboard candles, a specially covered book, mats. Children will soon find their own materials if they are helped to see the ordinary objects for liturgy in church or in school.

I remember in the weeks before my first holy communion, practising giving and receiving the 'host' with a packet of salt and vinegar crisps and wincing as the chemical flavouring burnt the roof of my mouth while I tried not to chew. Somewhere in our school I know we have a set of tiny vestments made by pupils many years ago, clothes that any Action Man would be proud to wear! Years ago I watched a little girl make a Mass set out of her tea service and line up plastic play people in front of her on the floor – and of course, she took the role of the priest.

Preparing liturgy

> Each [eucharistic] celebration with children should be carefully prepared beforehand ...

... especially with regard to prayers, songs, readings, and intentions of the general intercessions...

This should be done in discussion with the adults and with the children who will have a special ministry in these (Masses).. .

Over and above the appropriate internal participation, such activity will help to develop the spirit of community celebration.

DMC §29

Hands up if you have said in the last year 'I've got to go home and write my assembly tonight' or 'My class has got its assembly next week.' Change those statements to 'My class is preparing an assembly for next week' and you will have made a major shift in your thinking, one that could transform the way you approach liturgy at school.

The teacher must be prepared, not just in a practical way but spiritually too. There is no point knowing all the theory of liturgy without allowing it to affect your life. In the same way that people develop a love of music or art through personal response as well as knowledge, you need to foster a love of liturgy born from study and your own experience.

In guiding children in their preparation for liturgy the teacher needs to listen, wait, observe and guide but not be tempted to rush children into choices that are not their own. This will require time, patience and a re-moulding of deeply ingrained teaching techniques that so often rely on teacher talk and the transmission of knowledge. This transformation of relationship cannot happen overnight but should be in the teacher's mind when with the children for this task. Remember that to 'educate' means to 'draw out', not to put in.

Involving the children in the preparation, following an outline structure like that described later in this book, is vital if we are going to have celebrations that are sensitive to the lives of young people. Try not to be tempted into a theme and do not go to the bother of planning something from scratch – already the church gives us the formats and elements needed to do liturgy. About nine-tenths of the job is done for us, especially for Masses. What you and the children do is make that set of words and actions speak to your community in this time and place. Remember that the holy spirit is in the preparing and the doing too – liturgy is a live event, not a performance that has to be perfect.

Guide the children's choice

Won't the children come up with outlandish ideas?

Quite probably, yes! And it is your job to guide them into simple, clear and dignified choices in the same way you would if the children were planning a concert and wanted, as our Year 6 pupils do every year, to base it on recent scenes from Eastenders. It is your responsibility to say 'no' to some suggestions that do not fit comfortably with what you know of the feast, the readings and the people. Apply the skills of discretion and judgement that you use well in other areas of school life.

Listen to what the children have to say. Practise true listening, that does not interrupt or offer solutions before the speaker has had time to reflect. Be patient and wait. Most of us will know the experience of 'talking out a problem' – in describing our thoughts and finding that in thinking out loud with a friend we find the solution emerging without the advice of the listener. As teachers, we could all do with learning how to be more active listeners such as we need in an activity like Circle Time.

begin with the readings

Consider the season or feast that is being celebrated and begin with the given readings. Explore through discussion what those texts and thoughts mean to the children. Think of ways to enhance those thoughts in the liturgy without giving way to complexity or gimmicks. Write down the things that you need to prepare and tell the rest of the school or key stage what they might need to prepare for what is going to take place.

use bold symbols, clear language, moments of silence

Since each school has its own character developed over many years and altered by the different intakes, the job of the group doing the preparing is to devise a natural way of celebrating that is appropriate for all members of the group. This may feel a difficult task, considering the wide age range that could be present but if the liturgy uses bold symbols, clear language, moments of silence and is sensitive to all our senses it will provide that meeting place for God and God's people. Don't try to create a liturgy that is so watered down in text and built up in unnecessary commentary that no one is satisfied.

At St Mary's, we have separate Key Stage 1 and 2 assemblies each week which are prepared and led by one class. Some children from this class form the group of ministers – reader, cantor, musician, intercessor, leader – while the remainder of the class and rest of the key stage participate as the assembly. In this way, every child is involved in preparing liturgy up to three times a year. Since each assembly lasts for just 8-10 minutes and is centred around the reading of scripture, teachers are finding there is gradually less need for lengthy preparation and practice. We have left behind the 'production' assemblies and are beginning to move towards more simple, reflective liturgical assemblies.

Doing liturgy

[Liturgy] is the **right and duty** of all the baptised, both children and adults.

Guidelines, p 5

It cannot be expected that everything in the liturgy will always be intelligible to them . . .

Nonetheless, we may fear spiritual harm if over the years children repeatedly experience in the church things that are scarcely comprehensible to them: recent psychological study has established how profoundly children are formed by the religious experience of infancy and early childhood, according to their individual religious capacity.

DMC # 2

You will have read earlier that liturgy is not something done *for* children but rather a celebration *with* them. Now we are reminded that all of us, including children, have 'a right and duty to take a full, active, conscious part in liturgy because of our baptism.' Sometimes children are regarded as mini-adults waiting to grow up and be whole but we know they are each complete persons with real experiences of their own to bring to liturgy.

Note that it is everybody's full *participation*, rather than their compliant stillness and obedience or rigid movement that is called for.

If children are not participating in the responses, gestures and singing as you would hope, ask 'why not?' It will usually not be out of laziness but more likely out of too little preparation, confusion, lack of encouragement and example from the adults around them.

This role modelling is vital in schools. Ask yourself:

- would you do a PE lesson without demonstrating how to throw the ball?

- do you ask the children to write a descriptive passage without first leading a shared writing session?

- do you sit at the dinner table and not encourage the children to talk with their fellow eaters?

Why then is it OK for adults (and here I mean teachers, teaching assistants, admin staff, parents) to sit in the assembly hall and not show participation by example? In some schools, assembly time is non-contact time 'kindly' offered by the head teacher to her staff. In many schools the adults are there only as monitors, policing the children. I admit that we still need to encourage appropriate and safe behaviour from the children in liturgy and if someone is disruptive they need to be talked to but - during the assembly?

Children will always look at their teacher to know how to react when something new or unusual happens: when there is a visiting music group they look to staff to know when it is appropriate to clap, when someone trips over in the hall they look around them to the adults to know whether or not it's OK to laugh.

So too in liturgy, the children look round to the adults to know how to respond, how to sit, how to make the gestures of the church. They learn, as we all do, by observing and doing.

A natural routine

The act of doing liturgy should feel a natural routine for us all. The rituals should become so familiar that they come from our heart rather than our heads. Liturgy is not something done to us, it is something we do with others. If it is different every week, invented anew each time in the false belief that it has to be interesting, fun, instructional and lively then we have lost the connections with our past and future experiences and those of the wider church. Any hope of a solid foundation crumbles if you start from scratch each week, searching for new themes and gimmicks. Leave that to the entertainers and film-makers!

And remember that the spirit is in the doing as well as the preparation. It is easy to get caught up in doing the 'perfect' liturgy but that may not lead us to God. Things will inevitably not go to plan but those moments of 'disaster' are often the gifts from God pointing us towards unexpected understanding if only we are open to seeing them as such.

The ritual of our school assemblies remains very much the same week after week, year after year. If a class has prepared the liturgy those children form a circle in the middle of the hall with the focal point (table with candle, bible, cloths and other symbols) in the centre. The rest of the school forms concentric circles around the inner one. Everyone participates in the responses, the songs, the reflections, the gestures and the prayers. The structure of the liturgy is always **Gather – Proclaim - Respond – Leave**. We celebrate the same annual liturgies as a whole school, for example on Remembrance Day and the first Monday of Advent. Each year we may change one song or prayer but essentially the liturgy is largely unaltered and therefore familiar. Everyone begins to know the responses, gestures and songs by heart.

Is it possible to do 'bad' liturgy?

Good celebrations foster and nourish faith. Poor celebrations may weaken and destroy it.
Music in Catholic Worship, US Bishops, 1972

Liturgy with children, as with adults, demands dignity, clarity and simplicity.
Guidelines

God is not concerned with us doing liturgy according to a book, and Jesus would certainly have been the first to abandon the rules if they were not life-giving and inclusive of the whole community. The structures, gestures, symbols and words are there for our benefit and have been developed over many centuries. Learn to lean on the good things of the tradition and the wisdom of those who have gone before us.

Having said that we should certainly strive for liturgy to be done well, even though we know that it will never be perfect. Children learn about liturgy by doing, so their experiences should be good ones.

The way we do liturgy tells others what we believe about ourselves and our God. Everything we do during liturgy in the assembly hall or classroom – the way we sit, the way we welcome one another, the symbols, the art, the colours, the smells – should be invested with care, dignity and simplicity. Less is more. Avoid, for example, cluttered prayer tables heaped with every conceivable religious artefact.

Liturgy should not be an endurance test for those who have gathered, nor should it be a performance or a competition between classes. Some school assemblies come to resemble major West End productions with costumes, lighting, props and lengthy stories, with a short prayer clipped on at the end. The parents and other children are thanked for 'coming to watch our assembly' and clapping ensues.

I am not saying there is no place for these assemblies. but we should learn to recognise that they are not liturgies, and may be avoiding the encounter between God and people that could happen when the Word is proclaimed and a response given in a communal action.

Don't give poor example

We have to be prepared for children learning from poor example too. Poorly done liturgy can form misinterpretations. If a member of staff talks through the silence then the children have every right to believe that it is fine for them to whisper to a neighbour too. If an adult in the school does not join in with the singing of a response or song, then the children can rightly not participate too.

Our presence as adults is essential because liturgy is something people of all ages do, and of which children gradually grow in understanding. If it is always totally 'child-centred', at the 'children's level' etc., then when that child becomes a young adult she is likely to reject all of what the church is and could be for her. She will see faith as something just related to childhood. More and more, in many parishes, the time of confirmation is becoming a time when young people leave the church; only to return when they have children of their own to start school – effectively a leaving certificate.

Remember that all liturgy – both good and bad – forms us. We would hope that in schools the whole community can celebrate with creativity and richness.

If children listen to a peer stumble through a reading in a timid, hesitant voice with no understanding of the sentence markers, then that says that the reader is more important than the Word of God. If there are no real candles on the Advent wreath but paper cut outs instead that fails to help us to know Jesus as the Light of the World. If the overhead projector is the most prominent feature of the room then our eyes are drawn to that instead of the candle burning on a side table.

Training

Preparing and leading liturgy is a skilled job that requires training, study, reflection and practice if it is to be done confidently and well. Liturgy has long been neglected simply because no-one knew how to change it and the repetition of old patterns became comfortable. Many of us prepare assemblies that hark back to our own childhood school experiences without having the opportunity to reflect on whether or not they are good practice. Some schools have come to a point where they know they do not want to continue with their present pattern of 'competitive' class assemblies but do not yet know what to develop instead.

Teachers who have had a moving experience of liturgy, perhaps on a course or on holiday, return to school feeling that something is missing. There is certainly a deep desire in many schools for training and personal experience of good liturgy and this, of course, has implications for the diocesan and school INSET budgets especially if you decide to make liturgy a priority on the school development plan. We would not dream of embarking on an evaluation of any other area of the school without forward planning and financial commitment and so liturgy and the prayer life of the school demand that same close attention.

Making connections – feeling we belong

When we enter a situation that is unfamiliar to us, our first response is to find a way of connecting it to something we already know and understand. This is what we mean when we teach children to 'know what to do when you don't know what to do.'

With liturgy too we are faced with a number of new experiences and we use our skills of analogy to strengthen the connections with familiar past experiences which form a solid base for moving on. We feel we belong more and more as we become accustomed to the rituals we participate in. Keeping many elements of liturgy the same is vital for our understanding, sense of belonging and growth.

You may have watched some of the TV programmes on the brain presented by Professor Robert Winston. In one episode the professor gradually builds a structure to bridge the gap across a wide river. He begins by throwing across a rope. After several attempts the hook catches on the other side and the first contact between both sides is made. But it is a very unstable line. Bit by bit, more ropes are strung across the gap and planks of wood are placed across the rope to make a bridge.

When the scientist makes his first tentative journey from land to land the structure rocks viciously and the walker is notably shaken by the experience. But as he walks back and forth many times he is able to add structural strength, making each journey easier than the last. The comparison in the programme was with a brain's synapses growing to strengthen the connections needed to receive and retain new knowledge. To us the comparison could be with the strength of understanding that comes (indeed is necessary) with repeatedly celebrating the same liturgy. Taken a step further, the comparison could be with the connections between heaven and earth that are strengthened too.

5 The sights and smells of liturgy

Setting the scene

> Arranging the worship space is a ministry. It should be well-prepared before the children arrive. *Guidelines*

PREPARATION FOR LITURGY DOESN'T JUST INVOLVE THE WORDS OF READINGS, PRAYERS and responses. You will remember from chapter two that all of our senses are involved since we bring our whole selves. Here we will look at the environment for liturgy, considering in particular what we see and smell.

On teaching practice, and through painful experience, many of us will have learned that preparation is a vital element of a successful lesson. Having resources ready in advance frees us up to be concerned with the principal task of teaching.

The same applies when doing liturgy. Preparing the space in advance liberates us to participate fully in the experience and can be a prayerful act in itself. Children enjoy taking part in the practical preparations and will learn to understand the liturgy more through this role. Consider appointing a member of staff to keep the liturgical resources clean, tidy and in good repair. Items used for liturgy should be kept in a special place and not used for other purposes.

The place

> It should be a place where the children can conduct themselves freely according to the demands of a living liturgy that is suited to their age.... the place chosen should be appropriate and worthy. *DMC §25*

The principal place for liturgy is the **church**. Some schools share their site with the parish church and can easily walk the school community there regularly. Others find themselves a long way from the church and travel there only on a few occasions in the year. A small number of schools have been able to set aside space as a chapel or prayer room for small groups of children.

For most primary schools, though, the **hall** will be the place for assemblies since it is close by, suitable for the range of children and a familiar place for doing a school

community activity. While some schools have the luxury of two halls most will know that their hall also functions as a gym and a dining room - activities that both bring their own equipment and smells! How can we make the hall a place of worship? What does the space we use say about how we feel about each other and God?

Layout and seating

Churches have pews or lines of chairs that keep us in our places and can make us feel we are at a theatrical performance. The place that we celebrate in and the choice of layout deeply effect what we think about what we're doing. Remember that liturgy is about all the people together not about 'them doing something to/for us'. Think about the shape of your hall and the arrangement of the seating. Do the children feel as though they are here for a lesson or for something different? Do adults feel part of the group and not spectators? Can everyone see the focal point and lectern? Can people see each others' faces or only the backs of heads? Is there a sense of belonging in the way you sit? Who gets to sit on the chairs or benches? - it says something very powerful when children are given a choice over where they sit in the room or if a member of staff chooses to sit on the floor to pray.

Our hall is very small for the number of children on roll and is particularly squashed when we invite parents (and baby buggies!) to join us for celebrations. It is important that everyone feels comfortable and welcomed, so over about five years we have developed a number of seating arrangements for different occasions. The children are made aware of what is about to happen by the formation of the room and are very quick to understand the less usual patterns. Here are some of the arrangements we use throughout the year:

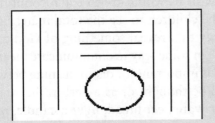 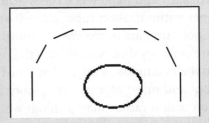

Weekly whole school assembly   Whole school assembly with parents

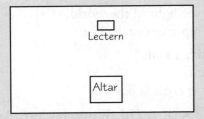 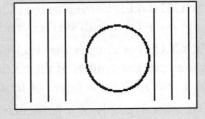

Mass with years 2-6   Key stage 1 or 2 assembly

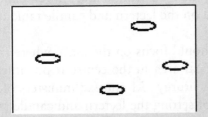 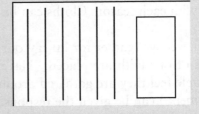

'Quiet' assembly with Years 3-6   Concert or play

Symbols

As with any language, the symbols are more or less arbitrary, yet they embody meaning, reveal attitudes, make possible a sharing of feelings and vision, and act as a vehicle of conversation.

The Welcome Table, p.33

Using visual objects in liturgy is something most teachers are drawn to, especially those whose classrooms are full of wonderful displays and practical tools to help children learn and experience the world. Few of us would try to teach counting to little ones without using cubes or beads for the children to see the total increasing.

Symbols are part of the classroom of liturgy that reveal something of God to us. They are ordinary domestic objects that we use in some way to communicate meaning beyond their common reality. That word 'use' is important for distinguishing between a symbol and other objects. A symbol could be thought of as a verb rather than a noun, an action rather than a thing: we *pour* water, *eat* bread, *light* a candle, *mark* with the cross, *sign* with ashes etc.

The principal symbols (or objects that we use symbolically) are:

❧ The **BIBLE** or lectionary, placed on a lectern (stand) or table.
We call this place 'the table of the word'

❧ The **CANDLE**, showing us that Christ is the light of the world.
Perhaps on a table with smaller candles to represent each class

❧ The **CROSS** or crucifix that is clearly visible to all.
This is an ancient symbol of the Christian faith
Note: a crucifix has the figure of Jesus on it, a cross is bare.

❧ The other symbols of a particular liturgy such as **Oil, Water, Incense, Ashes, Bread** and **Wine**

❧ Seasonal **COLOURS** that help us to focus on the mood of each season. You will notice that the colour of the priest's vestments, the altar frontal and church banners change with each season. Cloths can be draped on the lectern and candle table too.

Whenever we gather for liturgy our eyes should focus on the place where these symbols of our faith are placed. Have this focal area in the centre if possible, so that people feel they are gathered around it for liturgy. Monitors ('ministers of the environment') can be given the responsibility of setting the lectern and candle table in place each time, since these will probably need to be put to the side of the hall for PE lessons and lunch time. Children enjoy the responsibility of these tasks and learn so much about liturgy by doing them.

Will children understand all of the symbols? Not at once. That is the point. As with so much you have read in this book, liturgy is not an instant experience; we grow into it over a lifetime. If the symbols are large, worthy objects and are handled with reverence they will begin to speak by themselves. One day the symbols will reveal a meaning beyond themselves but that may take many years and is not a once in a lifetime revelation – it is a continuous process that doesn't end until we die.

Secondary objects

In addition to the visual elements that belong to the celebration and to the place of celebration, it is appropriate to introduce other elements which will permit children to perceive visually the great deeds of God in creation and redemption and thus support their prayer. The liturgy should never appear as something dry and merely intellectual. *DMC §35 -36*

> *School staff have a range of wonderful opportunities to enjoy their creative sides. Make use of these skills in liturgy*

Art and decoration are things that schools do so well. Every primary school has its gifted artists whose display boards bring delight, inspiration (and a little envy) to others. Some teachers and teaching assistants just have the knack of putting colours together, arranging a cloth with just the right folds, knowing when a picture is straight, and bringing out the central idea of a story in one image.

Most people nowadays do not have much chance to be artistic in a practical way except perhaps in decorating their homes. School staff, though, have a range of wonderful opportunities to develop and enjoy their creative sides. Make use of these skills in liturgy!

When you have made sure that the principal symbols listed above are most prominent and are clearly recognised, think about having some secondary ones:

 A **statue or icon** of the school's patronal saint, decorated for the feast day

 Banners, posters or display boards announcing the season of the year with a phrase from scripture as the headline

 Plants, pebbles, flowers, sand, earth, branches – a variety of **real natural objects**. Plastic flowers are not a rich inspiration for a living God!

 Smaller **pieces of art work** that reflect the readings and themes of the season

Symbols large enough to see

Everything we use for liturgy, symbols and secondary objects alike, should be dignified and worthy of its task in bringing us closer in relationship to God. A bowl of water should be large enough for all to see, cloths should be kept clean and ironed, plants and flowers need to be tended frequently. Avoid making the liturgical space cluttered in any way, however enticing it may be to have a collection of rosary beads, prayer books, religious pictures and holy water bottles. Keep the primary symbols large and distinct and don't let them be obscured by the secondary objects. Think about the purpose of each item in the context of the season and its symbolic meaning for the people gathered. Always aim for simplicity and clarity.

> We have a special cupboard set aside in the hall for our 'liturgy kit'. Here we keep the liturgical cloths, Advent wreath, Jesse Tree symbols, posters, candles, matches (never any in the box!), water bowl and jugs, incense sticks, the Easter ALLELUIA letters, altar cloths, wine, hosts, communion plate and cup and copies of liturgies that are returned to year after year. These items are only used for liturgy and remain in the cupboard until the season when they are needed. On view all the time in the hall is a wooden lectern with the seasonal colour draped on it, a large wooden cross as well as our decorative lectionary and small round candle table. Each class has a prayer candle to bring to assembly and light from one large candle. The lectern and table are simply put to the side for dinner and PE times but are always clearly visible.

Books and papers

> Since in liturgical celebrations the books too serve as signs and symbols of the sacred, care must be taken to ensure that they truly are worthy and beautiful.
>
> *Introduction to the Lectionary, §35*
>
> Books containing the word of God proclaimed in liturgy remind the hearers of the presence of God speaking to his people. *Guidelines, p 7*

We all need to know, by seeing and doing, that the Word is central to our lives as Christians. Remember God is as present to us in the proclamation of the word as in the eucharist. And because God communicates through the word, we treat it with dignity. See more about the Lectionary on p. 50. (There are several very beautifully bound lectionaries available – see resource list in appendix).

Make it a rule to read scriptural texts directly from the Bible or lectionary and *not* from a piece of paper or card. If necessary, clip the version of the passage into a decorated bible so that everyone is very clear that what is being proclaimed is special. Intercessory prayers, introductions and other words can be backed onto stiff card, using the colour of the season, or held in a decorated folder

> One school I visited has laminated a set of A4 cards with the school crest and a cross on. These cards are used in all their liturgies to fasten on scripture texts with paper clips. This allows the readers to see the same layout of words that they have been using to practise with and adds dignity and uniformity to the visual setting.

Lighting

Although most school liturgies will take place in the day time, you may be surprised how dim the hall can be without the electric lights on. Switch the main lights off or close the black-out curtains if you have them to darken the hall and provide only candle light. This really helps to make the hall a sacred space and leads us into prayer and reflection. The image of Jesus as the light of the world is obvious when you light one candle in a dark room. In addition to candles, think of using a lamp or coloured stage lights if you have them. Altering the normal lighting shows that we are gathering for liturgy, not for a PE lesson or to eat lunch.

Fragrance

As with the lighting, you should work on getting the hall to smell right for liturgy. Fragrant flowers can go some way towards achieving this but the symbols used by the church are incense and scented oil. (Incense had the very practical purpose of covering up the body odour of large numbers of people standing close together in a small room!)

Light an incense stick and put the blunt end into a plant pot so that it burns slowly during the liturgy. Pour water and a few drops of fragrant oil in the top dish of an oil burner (remember to blow out the candle underneath when you leave the hall.) Again, think of how the hall can smell of liturgy, not the sweat of a PE lesson or the dinner time food.

We ask a few children to walk around the hall for ten minutes or so before the start of the liturgy, each waving a lit incense stick (light the end from a match then blow out the flame so that the end is just glowing). One child, when doing this job, said: 'It smells like when my Grandad died in Portugal.' In a small way she is beginning to make connections between what we do in school and what happens in the wider church.

Making an entrance

On entering the place for liturgy we should know straight away that this time is different to other times of the week. Think about having two candle bearers standing either side of the door(s) to welcome people or place a bowl of water (a reminder of our baptism) nearby. For some whole school liturgies, you might drape the doorways with greenery, coloured cloths or banners to show everyone that what is about to happen is very special.

Look out for objects throughout the year. You may come across a wonderful water bowl in the Christmas sales that you will need to put away until Easter, or a length of purple ribbon at a summer market stall that will be just right for the Advent wreath. Once you start you'll find yourself spotting resources all the time.

Think about the cultural backgrounds of the children and staff. Use fabrics from other countries and look to have a variety of crosses in the school that reflect the universal church. Ask families to bring back items from holidays abroad.

With all your purchases, find out where the item was made. Since our liturgies urge us towards justice we should be concerned about the hands that made the things we use. There are many fair trade companies that can supply suitable materials.

6　The sounds of liturgy

ALL OF OUR SENSES ARE INVOLVED IN LITURGY, but the sense of *hearing* is perhaps the one that is present in every liturgy. We hear, speak and sing many different kinds of sounds in a celebration.

Language

Liturgy has its own style of language that needs to be learned and understood, in the same way that genres of fiction or poetry need to be taught and explored.

There are particular phrases and words that occur often in prayers and scriptures. Listen to the text of the opening prayers in church for the next few Sundays, or read them in the missal. You will find that the language is clear and readily understood although it needs to be appreciated as special 'God' language. There are some realities that can only be expressed in a certain way, using words that may not be everyday ones.

Most of the time, there is no need to *re-write* prayer texts for children, especially for those in key stage two. Perhaps the Literacy Hour in a Catholic primary school could include 'liturgy' as an extra genre? Children will not understand every word, but everyone, and this means all of us whatever stage of life we are at, grows into understanding as our liturgical literacy develops.

Repetition is very important: learning to say words which may at first be strange (even the Our Father has strange words), but which will gradually yield up their meaning over a lifetime. Always 'diluting' the text for children means they will never have a connection with what is spoken in the parish on Sundays or in the wider church of all denominations.

Always a biblical text

Every liturgy must include a biblical text since it is through the Word that God speaks to us and calls for us to respond. A Mass must always include the Gospel reading, although the other readings and the psalm can be omitted (DMC 42). At present the Catholic church in England and Wales uses the Jerusalem Bible for all readings except the psalms. Very often the Jerusalem translation may be suitable for use with older primary children, especially for Gospel readings.

What is the lectionary?

The lectionary is the book containing the readings used at Mass on each Sunday and feast day of the year. It is usually published in three volumes. The new year begins on the first Sunday of Advent with Year A following the Gospel of Matthew, Year B Mark, and Year C Luke. The Gospel of John is read during Easter time, some of Lent and Christmastide. The weekday lectionary is arranged in a two year cycle.

There are several US 'children's lectionaries' available in the UK although the Bishops' Conference of England and Wales has yet to approve any text.

The scriptural texts in a lectionary may be slightly different from those in a bible. The first words may have been edited to clarify the context. For example 'Then he spoke to them...' will be changed to 'After coming to Jerusalem, Jesus spoke to his disciples...'

The Gospel cycle
YEAR A Matthew (2008, 2011, 2014)
YEAR B Mark (2006, 2009, 2012)
YEAR C Luke (2007, 2010, 2013)
[JOHN: Eastertide, some of Lent some of Christmastide]

The advantage of using a lectionary over a children's Bible is that the lectionary gives a translation of the original rather than a paraphrase which may lose the central meaning of the Word. Shorter texts are not necessarily always the best for children. Look carefully at what is to be proclaimed and use your knowledge of the children you are with to decide which translation to use.

It is important to refer to 'proclaiming' the Word rather than 'reading' the Word since we believe that Christ is present in the Word as in the eucharist. When the Word is proclaimed we are breaking open the scriptures for all present.

And remember, as we mentioned earlier, the books that the texts are read from should be dignified and worthy of their task since they say to the people gathered that what they contain is very important to us.

Each year we celebrate a worship service with key stage 2 children, their parents and the staff, sharing the stories of Christmas through mime, dance and song. We used to read from a variety of paraphrased versions of the texts but now use the readings directly from the Jerusalem bible, as we hear them proclaimed in church.

Over the years these readings, with their particular language, have become deeply ingrained within us. Teachers involved with the preparations for this night can quote large passages off by heart. The children, especially those who have been readers in our worship, are able to 'grow into' the language over four years and are led into making connections with what they hear in the parish. Some classes spend time in their literacy lessons doing shared reading and writing tasks with these texts.

The readings help you understand how to be a better person. I must say the readings have helped me get more friends and and they have helped me keep them. — Jack

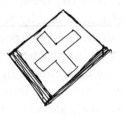

Can you hear me?

Many children's voices carry remarkably well in a large space. That is why children were often used in the ancient church to sing and read. It is very frustrating for everyone if speakers – children or adults - cannot be heard clearly.

Choose readers carefully and give them plenty of opportunity to rehearse in the liturgy space, not just in the classroom. Not everyone has the skills, confidence or desire to be a reader and no child or adult should be forced into this ministry.

Make sure the layout of the hall gives the shortest distance between speaker and hearers. A microphone will not always solve problems of poor diction or intonation and often generates technical problems of its own. If you are using a CD player make sure it is placed away from the focal point - it should not be a prominent feature of the room. And ask the kitchen staff to switch off the potato peeler - during assemblies ours always seems to start up in the silent moments!

Silence

Even in Masses with children 'silence should be observed at the proper times as a part of the celebration' lest too great a role be given to external action. In their own way children are genuinely capable of reflection. They need, however, a kind of introduction so that they will learn how to reflect within themselves, meditate briefly, or praise God and pray to him in their hearts. *DMC §37*

The dialogue between God and his people which happens through the power of the Holy Spirit requires short intervals of silence. *Guidelines*

Many teachers will know the experience of having that lasting silence that occasionally occurs in a classroom, a silence that cannot easily be broken. It is not an imposed quietness that might erupt into noise or giggles at any moment. True silence arises when the children are totally caught up in their task or are experiencing something awesome.

It is in the silence that the most profound moments of liturgy occur. There is a tendency, caused by nervousness, for adults who are leading a liturgy to talk through the silence and not rest in it. If you begin to think of silence as an active moment, not just an absence of sound then it becomes an integral part of liturgy. Playing instrumental music, humming a song or using sign language can help bring a group down from sound into silence. That way a tangible silence can be created rather than demanded. Ravel's orchestral piece Bolero ends with two bars of conducted silence to ensure that the audience and players acknowledge this essential and measured period of stillness.

As the adults in the school, we lead the children best by allowing the silence to be important for us. For many of us, being prayerfully silent on our own is difficult but when done in the presence of others it is a life giving and supportive act.

We have a 'quiet assembly' with each key stage about once a fortnight.
  Everybody, children and adults, enters the hall in silence and chooses to sit where they wish. Many sit in roughly concentric circles around the lit candles placed on large scattered cloths. Others move to the very edge of the room to be alone, others choose a chair or bench. The place is dimly lit and very quiet, with the smell of incense floating in the air.
After a short song or chant has been sung and a brief phrase from the Gospel has been proclaimed and some questions raised for us to ponder, we all sit in silence for up to three minutes. I have no idea what goes on the minds of the children but I do know that we can almost feel the silence and are able to leave with the knowledge that we have touched the spiritual.

On Wednesday we have a quiet assembly. When I'm in a quiet assembly it makes me feel relaxed and makes me put all bad thoughts aside. It also gives me time to think and pray. I find it easier to pray and feel more relaxed with candles, they help me to remember that Jesus is the light of the world.

- Antonia

Music

Since singing must be given great importance in all celebrations, it is to be especially encouraged in every way for Masses with children in view of their special affinity for music. *DMC §30*

This is such a huge topic it could take up another whole book! Music, especially singing, is absolutely integral for any liturgy since by singing together we are declaring our faith in each other and God. The church's liturgical documents talk about 'singing *the* liturgy' rather than 'singing *at the* liturgy', referring to the continuous musical response throughout a celebration.

Thankfully at many primary schools, there is still a culture of communal singing for religious as well as secular events although many schools feel that without a member of staff able to play the guitar or piano they need to rely on CD backing tracks to sing.

Schools in the secondary sector can be faced with a lack of enthusiasm for singing and no timetabled slot for practising new material for liturgy.

What we do with the younger children will profoundly effect their attitudes to singing in their future years as teenagers and later still as adults.

Singing in assembly makes me feel so relaxed and it wakes me up in the morning and makes me feel so alive
-Jobe

Singing confidence

Somebody once told me of a young girl long ago
Singing teacher told her she sounded like a crow
Fifty years went by until she sang again
All because those dreadful words stayed inside her brain.

Stephen Fischbacher, from song *Sticks and Stones*, on *Build Up* CD

I've got a terrible voice.

But I can't sing a note.

I'll put the children off.

Who told you these things? It makes me very sad when I hear stories from teachers who have been told by their own educators or by their families that they can't sing or that they sound awful. Such long-lasting damage has been done by these comments and, not only has that teacher lost out, but the children in his/her care have also.

> **Believe in the voice God has given you. It is the voice of an apprentice angel.**
>
> John L. Bell

Let everyone sing, regardless of the sound. The best way to improve your singing confidence is to sing often. As with visual artists, we would all acknowledge that there are those gifted from birth with beautiful voices but for most of us the way to develop our singing is by doing. If you find yourself singing out of tune, just tell others it's harmony!

The first sounds that babies make are an imitation of the musical intonation of voices. Only later do we develop speech.

Children, especially the younger ones, love singing and you'll hear them singing away in the playground and in the classroom. Getting the older children to sing can be difficult if they don't see it as an adult activity. By having all the grown ups in the hall join in the singing, the children see and hear that this is something worthwhile, enjoyable and for life.

> We have had members of staff come to our school declaring they 'can't sing a note' and yes, they have struggled to find the same pitch as everyone else but after a few years of singing in every music lesson and assembly they've got it.
>
> A staff singing group –with teachers, site manager, head teacher, admin staff, chair of governors and teaching assistants – has formed because we have discovered that singing is fun and brings us closer together. A second-ary effect has been to show the children that singing is done by adults too. A child, on hearing our first 'performance' during the Christmas worship rehearsal, commented: 'Well, you don't hear that every day.' Indeed!

Repertoire

Choosing and leading music is an important liturgical ministry. Thoughtfully chosen songs, chants and responses can deeply affect the prayer and participation of the people. Poor choices can result in a feeling of despondency.

When choosing what to sing, bear in mind that not all songs with religious lyrics are suitable as liturgical songs. Many were written as teaching songs or to retell a narrative story from the Bible. A liturgical song is different in that it has a specific purpose and often accompanies an event. It may give us a beat to walk to in a procession, be a response to a prayer, help to lead us into silence, be a reflection on the reading or bring about a sense of belonging. The liturgy does not stop for the singing of a song.

Your school's repertoire need not be large but should be varied enough to add richness to the liturgy, accompany each season and reflect the age and cultural groups gathered. Such a repertoire might include:

    ✺ songs for each season – Advent, Christmas, Lent, Easter – that are saved for use only at those times each year

    ✺ short songs - responses, chants, litanies and rounds

    ✺ longer songs - straight hymns with verse/chorus format

    ✺ fast songs – ones that can bring energy and a sense of joy at belonging

    ✺ slow songs – ones that can lead to reflection and express a range of deep emotions

    ✺ traditional songs – ones that can bring the children into the life of the wider church now and in the future

    ✺ modern songs – ones that echo the rhythms and melodies of today

    ✺ songs from a variety of cultures with some use of other languages

Think about the **text of the song**: Firstly, do you believe it? Would you sing it yourself? Does it reflect the beliefs of the church? Can the children be brought into an understanding of the overall meaning? Who is the song about? Is it addressing God or the people? Is the text dignified and worthy of liturgy?

Consider the **melody of the song**: Is it enjoyable to sing? (if not, the children will let you know very quickly!) Can it bear frequent repetition? Does it require accompaniment? Is the music dignified and worthy of liturgy?

The **way you use** the songs is often as important as the text and melody themselves. A small repertoire can be extended to fit a large number of liturgies and purposes whereas a large one can be a burden and never allows for repetition and depth. Have a range of songs for difficult occasions ready – there is no point learning a new song about hope in despair on the morning of a national disaster. What did you sing on 12 September 2001 or 8 July 2005? What will you sing if a child or member of staff dies?

Try using the chorus of a song on its own as a chant by repeating it four or five times, gradually reducing or increasing the volume. The response of a psalm can be sung while the verses are spoken over a piano accompaniment. Split the large group into two or three sections for singing a round or a 'call and response' song. Use different verses of the same song at various points throughout the one liturgy.

Learn as much as possible off by heart. There is nothing more tiring than having everyone sing continuously through six verses of a hymn. Have soloists ('cantors') sing the verse and everyone respond with the chorus. You will be amazed by the energy and volume with which everyone sings after listening. If you are using words on the wall, for example projected from the overhead or data projector, make sure the text is very large and there is an older child to point out the lines as they are sung. Learning to read a hymn, especially one with a chorus and verse format, is a literacy skill that needs to be taught. Spend time also rehearsing the beginnings and ends of songs so that everyone can enter into the singing with confidence right from the start.

Recorded music

Many schools do not have a pianist or guitarist on the staff and so rely on the use of pre-recorded backing tracks. If this is your situation try to also build in some time to sing unaccompanied. You may be surprised by the wonderful sound of your own voices and could begin to sing very short songs and litanies instead of a whole versified hymn.

The prayerful atmosphere in the hall can be aided by the use of recorded instrumental tracks. Consider your collection carefully so that it includes music from a variety of times and cultures. Ask children to bring in their own choices too that would fit the purpose. Will the music at the beginning be the same as at the end? What type of atmosphere can be created?

> It can take up to ten minutes for our whole school to process into the hall. Quiet music is often very suitable to encourage everyone to be part of creating the atmosphere for prayerful reflection. But sometimes, especially if we are gathering for a special occasion, we use CD tracks from our current music curriculum repertoire – anything from Handel to Glenn Miller or S Club7 - and the children join in with the words, signs and their own dance moves. This gives us all a very powerful sense of belonging which is an integral part of the gathering at the start of liturgy.

Live instrumental music

> The use of musical instruments may be of great help in Masses with children, especially if they are played by the children themselves. The playing of instruments will help to support the singing or to encourage the reflection of the children; sometimes by themselves instruments express festive joy and the praise of God. *DMC §32*

There are three main purposes for instrumental music in liturgy –
to accompany the singing,
to accompany an action,
to help create a specific atmosphere.

Much will depend on the musical opportunities that the children are given in school and the ability of teachers to enable instrumental music to be played confidently. Seek out children who have music lessons outside school. There may be a member of staff who plays an instrument very well and who could be encouraged to use this skill in a liturgy.

A descant recorder is excellent for leading singing as it is pitched an octave higher than the voice and is easily heard.

Both the piano and guitar provide very good support for singing too and can also provide musical pieces on their own. Other instruments should be chosen carefully with consideration for the ability of the player, the volume and quality of sound. Bagpipes are very loud!

Always take care that the musical sound should be dignified and worthy of the liturgy and don't let it become a performance that requires the 'audience' to applaud. Having children or adults play is not to be seen as a showcase but as a service ministering to the people and the liturgy. If listening to the music becomes an endurance test for the people then it is not suitable. If the melody reminds the people of an advert, a film or another unrelated occasion then it is not suitable either. Save those pieces and players for another occasion.

Cultural music

The culture of various groups and the capabilities of the children present should be taken into account.

DMC # 30

In a city school, it is likely that the children and staff come from families of a wide variety of cultures. This great richness, when shared with respect, curiousity and understanding can be brought to the full in liturgy. Not only can the languages and art of many countries be present, but songs and instrumental music too. Children are very responsive to sounds from cultures other than their own and will often move spontaneously in an appropriate way. Put on a fast Scottish jig and they will begin to skip, play them a slow Nigerian drum beat and they will bend their boies and stamp their feet. Ask the children to teach you songs from their home culture perhaps ones that are sung in other church traditions.

Look outside the cultures of your own school too to find songs from the whole world church. By doing this, you are connecting with people in many other situations and places, calling them brothers and sisters, and experiencing some part of their life. Children usually find learning words in an unfamiliar language much easier than adults because those parts of their brain are still very active. Practise the pronunciation out loud often by yourself before attempting to teach it – it is very hard for the children to undo a mistake once they have sung a wrong note or said a new word incorrectly.

Isabel

... and if you can't hear?

For those in our communities who do not hear or do not hear well, other sensory experiences are vital for participation and understanding.

The use of British Sign Language, the language of the deaf, has a very powerful effect in our school liturgies. Over many years we have built up relationships with deaf people from the local community who have come into school to teach us signing. In order to interpret or 'translate' words into BSL it is necessary to understand the meaning of the whole phrase in the context using a visual picture. You learn a lot about a person's theology by the way they choose to sign songs and prayers

BSL: 'Jesus'

7 The Movements of Liturgy

The development of gestures, postures, and actions is very important for Masses with children in view of the nature of the liturgy as an activity of the entire person [man] and in view of the psychology of children. DMC §32

SINCE LITURGY IS SOMETHING 'DONE' RATHER THAN WATCHED it requires *movement*, not just from a few specially appointed ministers but of all the people gathered. Liturgy involves our whole body not just the head. God is revealed through the ordinary activities of our human lives.

Posture

The ways in which we hold our bodies in liturgy each have a meaning.

We **stand** to show respect and draw attention to an important happening, for example when the Gospel is being proclaimed. We **sit** in comfort to reflect and to listen. We **kneel** as an action of sorrow and devotion.

Each posture needs to be spontaneous and to feel natural. These are actions which should become familiar to us, which children will learn from the adults around them when these postures are modelled with ease and reverence.

Postures do not need a stiff rigidity that must be 'policed' and exact. The word *formality* should be taken in the sense of 'giving form to' rather than emphasising the strict observance of rules. Children should never feel threatened in liturgy. Instead, we need to foster a relaxed and prayerful stance while leading them into a dignified and unified way of moving in liturgy that is recognised in the wider church and helps us to express who we are as worshipping Christians.

Just as when we were learning to eat with cutlery as young children we didn't stop eating with our fingers straight away, in liturgy too it may take time before children (and adults) can manage their bodies comfortably when using ritual movements and gestures. But as with so much we are reading here, what happens in childhood is vital for future spiritual development and a sense of belonging in the church.

Gestures and ritual actions

In addition to the way we hold our bodies there are specific gestures used in liturgy. The most common of these for catholic Christians is probably making the sign of the cross on the body.

Other gestures include:

᛫ the sign of peace

᛫ carrying the Bible or Lectionary in procession

᛫ opening our arms to pray

᛫ bowing our heads in reverence or prayer

᛫ marking our foreheads, lips and heart with the cross at the Gospel

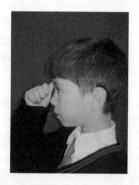

᛫ marking our foreheads with ashes on Ash Wednesday

᛫ laying on of hands

᛫ offering and receiving food

᛫ sprinkling with water

᛫ lighting a candle

᛫ putting a grain of incense onto burning charcoal

᛫ washing our hands with water

Simple gestures are part of life in general - we shake hands, give each other gifts, hold a door for one another. Using gestures in a particular context, and in a way that is unique to the liturgy, helps us realise that this is a special thing we are doing. Done with reverence, these gestures both create and reflect a state of mind.

If we find we are self-conscious about these actions we can draw strength from doing them with others. There may be a tendency to shy away from formal ritual movement in school, which is a loss for everyone. Done well and with full participation, the postures and gestures give form to the liturgy and help mould us. They do not make the liturgy a performance, if they are done in the right spirit.

Processions

• Entrance

By moving forward in procession during liturgy we show that we are a people whose faith does not stand still. Processions mark important moments in the liturgy that require our attention, and special days such as Candlemas and Palm Sunday.

The procession into the hall of the whole school can take many minutes but it should be a dignified, unhurried, purposeful and shared experience. The walking in says 'we want to be here, we belong and are glad about it.'

When I walk into the hall for assembly I suddenly feel like I'm in a different place. A quiet place. I then know that I have come to a place where I can be peaceful and pray without disturbance.

- Natalie

Perhaps each class could process into the hall led by an 'acolyte' holding the class candle which is lit from the main candle on arrival. Starting the opening song as people come into the hall highlights the fact that this should be a procession for everyone, not just the special ministers.

In school we have a chance to make the procession what it should be – the whole assembly gathering together. (Unfortunately this is rarely seen or understood in the church. Think about what happens in the parish on Sundays – the opening procession usually only involves the clergy and altar servers, the communion procession is so often the 'communion queue', more akin to a traffic jam.)

• Gospel

Those who are going to read the word of God should be given time to rehearse the procession from their place to the lectern and back again. Holding the Gospel book high shows the special honour we give to this book and moment.

• Final

The liturgy concludes with the procession out of all those assembled (again, not just those with a special ministry that day).

• Music for processions

Music should accompany these processions. An instrumental piece or a song with a refrain that can be sung from memory work well as sounds to move to. The intensity of the song will increase as more classes come into the place of worship and decrease as each class departs. It's a challenge for the last remaining group of children to keep the song alive till the end!

Every September our new reception children spend many minutes of their first weeks with us outside following the teacher along the straight lines of the playground. Behind is the teaching assistant shepherding those who have wandered off on their own. By the end of the month those little ones have learned how to 'process' and so can get to a lot of places. In an unhurried and safe way, they go to the school library down the corridor, they line up for their lunch, they move into the hall for PE. They know, however, that when they process with their hands joined ready for prayer they are going into the hall, not to eat or roll on the mats this time, but to do liturgy. No one tells them all this but they work it out for themselves by being led and by doing.

61

Actions to songs

Young children are very used to putting simple actions or movements to songs and we know this helps them to anticipate and understand the words they are using. In liturgy too it is very appropriate to use actions to songs and prayers as a way of involving our whole bodies and internalising the meanings. Standing up, swaying, clapping, clicking fingers, holding hands – all these are ways of enhancing our singing. Often children compose these for themselves and can offer to share their creative ideas with the whole school. The teacher doesn't have to do it all! For many, especially the visual and kinaesthetic learners, sign language, actions and movements help to remember texts much more easily than if they were reading them from the page. (see p. 54 for more about sign language.)

BSL: Friend

Dance

The purpose of dance in liturgy is to enable all those assembled to reflect on scripture and to turn us towards God in prayerful response. Often a small group will be given the ministry of dance, and the language which surrounds their movements should avoid any reference to performance or personal ownership. 'Year 2 will now perform their dance for us to watch.' 'Let's say well done to year 5 by giving them a big clap.'

The children will come to know of the power of their dance to move others to prayer when there is a deep silence following the closing chord of the music. The aim is for those surrounding the dancers to be drawn into the story, the emotions and the prayer.

Of course, dance could involve the whole assembly. Processions can turn into dances when music and movement combine in rhythm. A song used as a prayer response can draw everyone into dancing. Actions, signing and gestures all accompanied by singing lead to dance. The home cultures of your children will determine the genre of song and style of dancing most comfortable to the school community.

On an INSET course for the RE co-ordinators in Westminster diocese, the head teacher of a local primary school brought a group of year 6 children to lead a session on liturgical dance. For the whole two hour session we, the participants, sat in a large circle around the dancers to watch and listen. Even though we did not get to our feet to dance ourselves, we were all profoundly moved by what we saw. The children's bodies and faces were totally engrossed in the stories they were telling. Huge black cloths were use to create a dark tunnel through which hungry bodies crawled, pleading to be fed. Thin red and orange cloths were twirled in a vigorous dance for Pentecost. All of the teachers present that day will recall the deep effect on them. We were drawn into the event by watching and in no way felt excluded. This was not a performance.

These children, equal numbers of boys and girls, had been dancing and watching dances for their whole school lives so by the time they were 10 or 11 they had no sense of embarrassment but clearly a deep understanding of what they do and many skills in moving to music.

Of course, on return to my own school I immediately tried to replicate what I had seen with inevitably disappointing results initially. Dance in liturgy is relatively new to us and will take many years to develop strongly. The children have, however, created a number of very simple dances: one to show the emotions of the different characters in the Christmas story using large coloured cloths to wrap around them (fear), hold high in the air (happiness), fling on the ground (anger) and cover their heads (shame), and another to help those watching to reflect on the chorus of an Easter song which reads 'When people are cruel it makes all the difference to know where you're going and where you've come from.' (Fischy Music)

63

8 The Ministries of Liturgy

> The principles of active and conscious participation are in a sense even more valid for Masses celebrated with children. Every effort should be made to increase this participation and to make it more intense... In all this one should keep in mind that external activities will be fruitless and even harmful if they do not serve the internal participation of the children.
> DMC §22

MINISTRY OR 'SERVICE' IS SOMETHING THAT IS ALREADY DONE WELL in many primary schools. As children move up the school they become monitors or perhaps class reps for the school council. Older children like to help out in the nursery and those who find lunch times very long may offer to serve in the dinner hall by preparing drinks or wiping tables. Children love to help! You will know from your life in school that there is never a shortage of willing volunteers to take a message or fetch a pile of books.

Jobs for everyone?

Some teachers' main concern when preparing a school assembly is to find a job for each of the children in the leading class. Sadly this can lead to a misconception amongst both children and adults that cries:

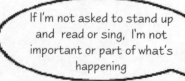

If I'm not asked to stand up and read or sing, I'm not important or part of what's happening

Of course there are special jobs that need to be done, but the basic truth is that we *all* participate by listening, singing, sharing gestures, reflecting and praying. Not

everyone will be called upon to get up and do something alone. The members of the class that has prepared the assembly may all have been involved in the preparation, but not all of them will be special ministers during the liturgy.

If children can learn to appreciate the roles of different ministries they will be able to understand one of the primary differences between liturgy and performance. This knowledge may also lead them to take their place as ministers in the Sunday church too, now and in the future as adults.

Each minister is entrusted with responsibility by the whole community and has a duty to prepare well for the role. In school it may be better for a child not to take on many different ministries, as each one needs time to prepare for.

A ministry should be carried out in such a way that the minister is not as important as his or her actions and what these actions point towards. It is never a self-centred act but a gift of yourself to God and others, which allows times of serving as well as being served.

What are these ministries we are talking about?

1 • The Assembly

IMPORTANT. Here we mean the **group of people,** rather than the event.

Everyone is a minister to everyone else gathered in the space – we are the Body of Christ, present in the world. Simply by being alive, breathing and present we are all 'ministers of the assembly'.

> These [adults] should be present not as monitors but as participants, praying with the children and helping them to the extent necessary. *DMC* §24

All children and adults gathered in the hall for liturgy are of equal importance and the arrangement of the room should enhance this belief rather than make us think we are at a show. The relationship is one of equality before God in this place, rather than one of pupil and teacher, as it may be in the classroom. All staff should be present as members of the assembly. Liturgy should never be offered as a 'gift' of non-contact time.

Be aware that older children too lead the younger ones by their actions, attitude and participation. Children at primary age use up a lot of time and angst making friendships and establishing their social groups. Peer example and approval is vitally important for security and growth at this age. Everything you learned about child development and psychology can be applied in this context. Be confident in your skills as a teacher and lead the children you are with by your own involvement.

2 • Specific ministries

From the body of the assembly some people step forward who have been prepared to carry out a defined ministry. They will have carried out this ministry many times and be known for the ease with which they carry out their role.

Leader

In the church context this ministry of leading would be the priest's or deacon's. In school, this ministry can belong to a member of staff or a child. On some occasions it may be appropriate to have more than one leader, perhaps for the different parts of the liturgy. Those taking on this role need to be very clear that it is one of service not one of being 'top dog'. The Gospel reading of Jesus washing the disciples feet with endless care should bring to mind the right approach.

Reader

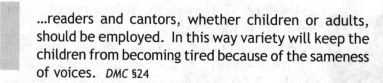

...readers and cantors, whether children or adults, should be employed. In this way variety will keep the children from becoming tired because of the sameness of voices. *DMC §24*

This is perhaps the most common ministry in schools. But in fact only some children and adults are suitable for this ministry and no-one should be asked to read the scriptures unless they are confident and very willing to do so.

The temptation is to make everyone in the class a reader by giving each a short sentence to say. But splitting the liturgy up into many sections or going home to write extra parts so that there are thirty snippets to be read aloud is not the way.

We usually refer to the reader as the person who has the ministry of proclaiming the scripture. (For the person who reads the invitation to prayer see *intercessor*).

The reader should have an understanding of the text and be given time to read it silently and aloud at home in order to communicate it well to others in liturgy. All the skills of public speaking apply – eye contact, pauses, clarity of diction, good volume, varied inflection – as well as the desire to bring others to God, remembering that God is present to us in the spoken word.

Some readings lend themselves to dialogue and narration which would involve several readers but avoid turning the proclamation of a text into a play with costumes and props.

Spontaneous mime can help bring the text alive with a group of children.

Intercessor

Those given the ministry of leading the people's response in prayer are the intercessors. The same person may have written the invitations to prayer. This phrase is important: the words are an *invitation* to prayer, not the prayer itself, beginning with a phrase such as:

Let us pray for…

May the school always…

i.e. they are directed to the people, not to God (unlike the prayers themselves, which everyone makes individually and silently). More is said about this in the next chapter.

Cantor

The cantor is a solo singer who sings the verses of the responsorial psalm and leads other songs by singing verses or responses. Some children are very confident in this ministry and, given encouragement and time, will lead others to prayer in a very powerful way. A few children can join together to form a group of cantors if none is able to sing alone.

When singing the psalm the cantor should use the lectern if you have one. Other songs needn't be sung from the front and are often very effective when sung from the back or simply from where the cantor is sitting with her class.

We have a fairly small number of cantors who each have their own song. Whenever that song is to be used in a liturgy, that child knows he or she is the soloist which means there is less need for rehearsal and the song is sung with great ease. Often it is the child who has taught us the song who always remains, in some ways, the owner of that melody. Of course, as the year 6 children leave their songs have to be inherited by the younger ones who are always eager to volunteer their voices!

Choir

Everyone in the assembly is a singer but some are called to be cantors or to support the people's singing by being part of a choir. The choir members can help sustain the main singing lines, can enrich the melodies by adding harmonies and may lead others to reflection by singing pieces on their own. A choir song should never be seen as a performance during liturgy and the young singers in school will need guidance to understand the different functions of each of their songs.

We rarely have a small group sing on its own and prefer to have everyone sing in liturgies, using the ministry of cantor more frequently. When we have used the choir to sing an individual piece we've struggled with finding a place for them to stand together and yet not be as prominent as they would be at a concert performance. To the front but off to one side can work well as can singing from the back, unseen.

Instrumental musician

Again, it is crucial to understand that the ministry of playing a musical instrument is one of service, not performance. A member of staff or perhaps a talented pupil may be able to accompany the singing on a piano or guitar. This requires practice and sensitivity so that the sound produced supports but does not overpower the singing. A sensitive accompanist will be able to vary the volume to direct the mood of the singing.

Make the introductions and interludes to every song the same each time, so that the singers can anticipate their entries with ease. And you don't have to play throughout the whole song: consider not playing for some verses, so that the singing can be fully heard.

The humble descant recorder is a much scorned but most useful instrument in school to lead the singing. Children's voices are able to follow the leading melody of this instrument although it can also be used to embellish the tune. A range of other instruments may also be available to you but not all will be suitable for accompanying voices. Some, when played solo or in small ensembles, can lead others to reflection and prayer through quietness.

Server

We are accustomed to seeing altar servers, both male and female, at church for celebrations of the Mass but this ministry is also essential in school liturgies. The server may be called upon to light candles, burn incense, pour water into a bowl, put ribbons on the Advent wreath or any number of other tasks. The server, more than any other minister, usually understands his or her role most deeply because it so clearly involves practical service for others.

Dancer

You will have read a bit about dance in liturgy in the chapter on movements. Those with this ministry need time and space to rehearse their part and to learn that dancing in liturgy is about bringing others to God, doing something on behalf of others. The contrast with performance should be pointed out and the expectation for applause discussed so that the children do not feel that their efforts have been dismissed or criticised in any way.

Welcomer

In many Catholic churches the congregation is large and spreads over several Masses during the weekend. It is unlikely that everyone will be familiar to you unlike the Sunday experience of worshippers in other denominations who gather in smaller numbers. When visiting an unfamiliar church it may be comforting to have someone welcome you at the door, perhaps with a hymn book and simply saying 'Good morning.'

In school, we all know each other at least by sight and so the need to have a welcomer is not so pressing. However, when inviting parents to participate in a liturgy it would be very appropriate to have a number of children at the school gate to greet those arriving and show them to the hall. At each door there may be further welcomers to hand out any service sheets being used and help parents, especially those with young children in buggies, find a comfortable place to sit. It has also become the role of our welcomers to ask people not to use mobile phones and cameras.

9 The shape of liturgy

A fully Christian life cannot be conceived without participation in the liturgical services in which the faithful, gathered into a single assembly, celebrate the paschal mystery. Therefore, the religious initiation of children must be in harmony with this purpose. *DMC* §8

T HE PASCHAL MYSTERY – THE DEATH AND RESURRECTION OF JESUS CHRIST - is the theme of *every* liturgy that we celebrate. Each time we gather we look again at this truth, approaching it from a different pathway.

Sometimes we highlight the forgiveness of God, or God's unending compassion for us in times of crisis and sorrow. At other times we celebrate the greatness of God through praise and thanksgiving. But all of these revolve round the central, eternal theme of salvation. Every liturgy that we prepare must have the paschal mystery as the root and centre.

Learn from history

Over the nearly two thousand years of the life of the Christian church, liturgy has acquired a shape. This is what we must learn and use. When you are preparing liturgy, don't start from scratch but use what is already there.

This doesn't mean that there is no work to do. Each liturgy needs to be adapted to the *particular assembly* that is gathering and it is important that you know the people, the place, the time and the reason for celebrating. And Liturgy takes time to be learned; it cannot be simply lifted off the page and 'done'. There is no such thing as an instant liturgy and books making such a claim should be left on the shelf.

The shape (or structure) of liturgy which has developed over the centuries is not an alien one unrelated to anything else we know. It is rooted in our lives as social human beings. The basic format: *we gather - we proclaim the word - we respond to the word - we leave* is that of many of our secular social gatherings.

Think of having friends round for an evening. People arrive and settle, coats are taken, drinks offered and there is a time of relaxing and catching up on recent news. The meal and wine provide the nourishment followed by a time of deeper talk, reflection, revelation and laughter. After comfortable, lingering conversation the moment of departure can come swiftly as guests realise the late hour, reach for coats, car keys and train tickets and say cheerio. All who have been present are in some way changed by the experience of the evening and may be leaving with thoughts or inspiration for their own lives.

We Gather

The introductory rite of the Mass has as its purpose 'that the faithful coming together take on the form of a community and prepare themselves to listen to God's word and celebrate the eucharist properly.' DMC §40

The free use of introductory comments will lead children to a genuine liturgical participation, but these explanations should not be merely didactic. DMC §23

Opening responses

Leader: We come together to pray –
All: **in the name of the Father, and of the Son,
and of the holy Spirit.
Amen.**
Leader: O God open our lips
All: **And we shall praise your name**

Opening words   (...brief introduction/context/season...)

Song

Opening Prayer (...use from missal for season or compose your own...)
Leader: O God...
You... Your...
Give us/guide us/watch over us/help us/make us/lead us
May we...
We ask this through Jesus Christ our Lord

All: Amen

The opening responses, leader's comment, song and prayer help us to gather together as a community, greet one another, acknowledge God and prepare to listen to the word. The leader may use familiar language in the brief opening comments but the liturgical language of the greeting and opening prayer should be retained. Remember when speaking that liturgy is not a time of instruction or explanation, although we may learn and be formed during it.

The introductory rites of a Mass have a number of additional elements. Either the penitential rite or the rite of sprinkling with water are used and then the Gloria (but not during Lent or Advent). It may be appropriate to use one or other of these in a school Liturgy of the Word, depending on the readings and season. An entrance procession involving everybody, assembly, leader, candle-bearers and readers - may also be suitable on special occasions.

Good beginnings are vital for worthy liturgy. They should not be overlooked or hurried, just as we wouldn't rush a guest straight from the door to the dinner table.

We Proclaim

Depending on the capacity of the children, the Word of God should have a greater and greater place in these celebrations. In fact, as the spiritual capacity of children develops, celebrations of the word of God in the strict sense should be held frequently, especially during Advent and Lent. These will help greatly to develop in the children an appreciation of the Word of God. *DMC §14*

Invitation

Reader: Let us listen to this reading from the Bible

For readings other than the Gospel

Reader: A reading from ...

After the reading

Reader: This is the word of the Lord
All: **Thanks be to God**

For Gospel readings

Reader: A reading from the Gospel of Saint...
All: **Glory to you, O Lord**

After the Gospel reading

Reader: This is the Gospel of the Lord
All: **Praise to you, Lord Jesus Christ**

At Mass the readings are sometimes viewed as a poor relation to the eucharist, something to be got through before the real thing begins. The Liturgy of the Word is of equal importance and as much care should be taken with it as the Liturgy of the Eucharist.

• What to proclaim

Every liturgy should centre around at least one text from the Bible.

At Sunday Mass the usual sequence is: Old Testament

Every liturgy should centre around at least one text from the Bible

reading, Psalm, New Testament reading then Gospel; but this will be too much in a school Liturgy of the Word. If there is to be only one reading, it should be from one of the four Gospels. Look at the readings prescribed for the day or season as your first source as these will often be very suitable. We use the Gospel reading from the Sunday Mass when we gather for a whole school assembly each Monday.

Be aware that the books of the bible contain many different genres of writing - letters, narrative, poetry, song lyric, revelation, history, instructions and so on – since this may colour the way you prepare the readers for their ministry. Non-scriptural texts (poems, stories, personal writings) may find a place in liturgy but must never replace the word of God.

> We have readings in our assemblies and I think the stories are a bit like our lives. They remind me of how things can be hard and easy in life. The more I listen to the stories about Jesus, the more they make me believe in him and what he had to do. It also makes me think that Jesus did things for us that he didn't want to do. The readings are very helpful and calm us down to make us understand.
>
> -Antonia

● Where to proclaim from

The Word of God should be proclaimed from a bible or lectionary rather than from a sheet of paper. You may consider having a lectern to place the bible on and a candle near the bible will help those assembled know that this is a special book.

● Who should proclaim

In a church setting at Mass, an unordained member of the assembly can be called to proclaim the scriptures of the old and new testaments except the Gospels. Only an ordained member (priest or deacon) may proclaim the Gospel. However, in a school setting in a liturgy of the word style assembly where no ordained minister is present, a child or adult may proclaim the Gospel. This is a tremendous responsibility, especially when we consider that we believe Christ is present in the word as in the eucharist.

A teaching assistant, a member of the Greek Orthodox church, who was asked to read part of the Gospel account of Jesus washing the disciples' feet at our school Holy Week reflection, commented on what a privilege it was to be given this role. She clearly knew the seriousness of what she was called to do and influenced other members of staff who were preparing to read their own passages from the passion narrative.

• Drama and mime

The liturgy is not a time for costumed dramatisations of the texts. This can happen in a concert, in the classroom, or at another assembly when the focus is on understanding the historical events. In liturgy, God speaks to the assembled people here and now through the Word. It is about us living in this time and place. Some movement or simple mime may help in the visualisation of the narrative and this is best done with no preparation at all in order to avoid the anxiousness of performance.

In some assemblies we read a passage once then invite some children to come forward to take on the roles of the characters. The children interact silently with each other in the centre of the hall, responding to the text as it is read for the second time. We ask the other children and adults to think about which character they are most like and what God is saying to them personally through the text.

No rehearsal is involved, but in this simple way the scripture comes alive for us today, and is not simply a good moral tale from the past.

• After the reading

In our school we often say: 'Let's listen to that again,' and proclaim the same passage for a second time to allow the words to settle. At other times we invite those present to choose one phrase or sentence that they can comprehend to ponder and recall throughout the day.

A brief explanation of the reading's context or a clarification of the identity of the characters may be needed before the proclamation but a lengthy exposition afterwards will reduce the proclamation of the Word of God to a literacy lesson. Instead the leader can invite those present to reflect on what the reading means for them.

It is not the role of the leader to tell everyone what the word should mean to them. It is God, through the word of his Son, inspired by the Holy Spirit, who is present and speaks to each of us. Let the Word speak, as it does in ways that you as leader may never know. The texts can never be fully explained; they are only understood over many years through imagination, eflection, experience and the making of connections.

It is important to allow a space for silence to allow the word to resonate. It is in silence that the principal relationship of child/God can become active. The leader should develop the humility to not interfere with this communication. We are all, young and old, children of the one God.

Emma

We Respond

RITUAL ACTION
(...different in each liturgy...)

INTERCESSORY PRAYER

Introduction

Leader:	A	We know that God loves us, so let us pray for ourselves and for others.
or	B	We are God's family, filled with the Holy Spirit, together let us pray.
or	C	Jesus has told us to ask God for what we need, so as God's children we pray.

Intentions

Intercessor: We pray for...
the church/ the world/those in need/local
        community/sick/deceased
        May they/it....

Reader: Lord, in your mercy
All: **Hear our prayer**

Or We pray to the Lord
Lord, hear our prayer

Or We pray to Christ the Lord
Christ, hear us.

Concluding Prayer

Leader:	A	Loving God, we ask you to listen to these prayers which we bring to you today In the name of Jesus the Lord.
All:		**Amen.**
or	B	Father, may your love be with us always and bring peace and joy to our families. We ask this through Jesus Christ our Lord.
All:		**Amen.**
or	C	God of tender love, you always hear our prayers. We ask you to grant us what we need, through Jesus Christ our Lord.
All:		**Amen.**

Ritual Action

The response to the Word may lead into a time of ritual action or communal prayer. The ritual action may vary, and may include all or some of the assembly in a practical way. Usually our senses are used at this point in the liturgy, especially the sense of touch.

Here are some examples of ritual actions throughout the school year:

Liturgy	Ritual Action
Start of the school year	Blessing the class candles
Harvest	Placing candles on world map
Remembrance Day	Bringing forward cards with names of the dead
Advent	Decorating and blessing the Advent wreath
Prayer for peace	Pass globe around while praying
Candlemas (Presentation)	Lighting candles from home and school
Ash Wednesday	Burning palms, signing with ashes
Beginning Lent	Hiding letters of ALLELUIA
Reconciliation	Pouring water over hands
Times of Fear and Mourning	Holding onto a pebble
Easter	Welcoming back the ALLELUIA
Pentecost	Marking foreheads with oil
End of school year	Coming forward to take a seedling

Intercessory prayers

Prayers happen at this point because God wants us to place our needs before him, and the best time to do so is in the light of the Gospel we have just heard.

They begin with an introduction by the leader and are directed to the assembly. The intentions that follow are *invitations to prayer* and the response is directed to God.

It can work well to have one reader for the intention and another for the response – this allows for a more measured pause of at least ten seconds in which people can pray. The Litany of intercessions ends with a concluding prayer.

These prayers are not letters to God or prayers beginning 'Dear Jesus...' nor are they intended as news bulletins, adverts or notices. Any important information should be given in the preparation time before liturgy begins. It is unfair to 'shock' people by making the initial announcement of a death or world event in these prayers.

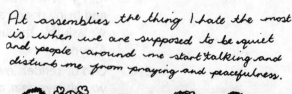

At assemblies the thing I hate the most is when we are supposed to be quiet and people around me start talking and disturb me from praying and peacefulness.

Natalie

For many of our whole school liturgies we give each class or year group the responsibility of composing a prayer intention on a given subject for example: 'for the sick' or 'for our local community'. Just as in a shared writing activity, the adult models the format of this genre of writing and invites groups of children to compose their own. One prayer intention is then brought to the liturgy and read by a member of that class who simply stands up in his/her place in the hall without coming to the front. Sometimes we have one older child who sings or says the response for all the prayers. This child can control the amount of silence allowed after each intention.

We Leave

Blessing

Leader:	May God, who (...*interject seasonal phrase* ...) bless us
All:	**In the name of the Father**
	and of the Son
	and of the Holy Spirit.
	Amen.

Dismissal

Leader:	Our celebration/assembly/time of prayer has ended.
	Let us go in the peace of Christ
All:	**Thanks be to God**

Song

The dismissal and blessing are short and, as with the other parts of the structure, do not need explanation. We simply acknowledge the presence of God with us and go forth, changed by the experience we have had together. The words of the blessing can be taken from the church's liturgy of the day (found in the missal) or composed by the leader.

We used to end every class led assembly with clapping, a response that we knew in our heads wasn't appropriate but was nonetheless our spontaneous reaction. In using silence more consciously and in following a ritual pattern for our liturgies we now feel in our hearts, as well as our minds, that clapping isn't what we want to do. We have not been at a performance with the parents and other children as the audience. We have been doing liturgy together as one assembled body.

10 The Time for Liturgy

The Calendar

IN EACH PERIOD OF TWELVE MONTHS WE BEGIN MANY 'NEW' YEARS. The calendar year begins in January, the financial year in April, the school year in September. To that list we could each add our own 'years' - marking time with birthdays, anniversaries of deaths, marriages, school foundations, house moves and so on. Thankfully this pattern of new beginnings allows us many moments in the year to reflect, renew and look forward. A resolution made on January 1st is rarely still unbroken by Easter and needs frequent renewal to keep it alive in our minds, recognising the many deaths and resurrections in our lives.

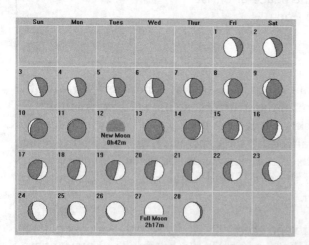

The church's liturgical cycle gives us one more way of marking each period of twelve months. It follows the natural seasons of the earth and moon in the northern hemisphere, beginning in winter on the 1st Sunday of Advent which falls sometime between the last week of November and the first week of December. The weeks of the year are arranged in seasons with Easter being the highpoint.

The Liturgical Year

Note: The Triduum is the central point of the church's year and all liturgical documents would place these three days at the beginning of any description of the cycle. On the next two pages is the chronological sequence:

Season of Advent Vesture colour: Violet with rose on the 3rd Sunday	• **Begins** on the Sunday four weeks before 25 December • There are four Sundays in Advent • A season of waiting, preparation and expectation • The first section up to 16 December is a time of expectation for Christ's second coming at the end of time. The second section looks towards celebrating the birth of Christ
Season of Christmas Vesture colour: white/ gold/silver	• **Begins** on Christmas Eve and ends on the Feast of the Baptism of Our Lord, which is the Sunday after the Epiphany • An extended time of reflecting on the meaning for us of Christ's birth
Ordinary Time Vesture colour: green, with white on feast days	• **Begins** on the first Sunday after the Baptism of the Lord (mid-January). • Not a season as such but a period of marking the weeks between the seasons of Advent/Christmas and Lent/Easter The first period includes the Feast of Candlemas (the Presentation of the Lord) on February 2, forty days after Christmas Day • 'Ordinary' as in counting, not plain or uninteresting. Weeks are named after the ordinal numbers e.g.1st, 2nd, 3rd • A time of hearing the scriptures unfold week by week with a continuous reading of one of the Gospels, chapter by chapter • There are three yearly cycles for the Sunday readings: Year A is Matthew, Year B Mark, Year C Luke • The weeks are counted from number 2 until Lent begins, then break off and resume after Trinity Sunday

Season of Lent Vesture colour: Violet with rose on the 4th Sunday and red on Palm Sunday	• **Begins** on Ash Wednesday and ends on the evening of Maundy Thursday • There are 40 days, six Sundays in Lent (thought to mean 'length' – the days of spring are getting longer) • The fourth Sunday is Mother's Day in the UK, the sixth Sunday is Palm Sunday • A time when the unbaptised (catechumens) prepare for their baptism at the Vigil on Easter Saturday night and the whole community recalls its baptism by fasting, praying and doing acts of charity • The word 'Alleluia' (Praise to God) is not used
Paschal Triduum 'Easter Three Days'	• The three days from sunset on Maundy Thursday, through Good Friday and Easter Saturday to the sunset on Easter Sunday • This is the centre of the church's year from which all the other seasons flow
Season of Easter **'Eastertime'** Vesture colour: white/gold/silver, with red on Pentecost	• **Begins** on the evening of Easter Sunday and ends on Pentecost Sunday when we celebrate the gift of the Holy Spirit to the church and each of us (sometimes called Whit (*white*) Sunday although red vestments are worn on this day now) • There are 50 days, a week of weeks plus one day = the time of eternity • Gospel readings are taken from John, first readings are a sequence of readings from the new testament Acts of the Apostles (instead of the old testament) • The symbols of water, light and fire prevail with a decorated Easter candle given most prominence • The word Alleluia is sung as frequently as possible
Ordinary Time Vesture colour: green with white on feast days	• The weekly counting of the Sundays resumes after Trinity Sunday (which is one week after Pentecost Sunday) and ends before the first Sunday of Advent
Advent	The cycle begins again...

Holy Days of Obligation

There are also special days that usually fall in the academic year, some of which are special days when the church invites/obliges us to participate in the Eucharist:

- ♦ All Saints   November 1
- ♦ Epiphany   January 6
- ♦ Ascension   Thursday 10 days before Pentecost Sunday
- ♦ Corpus Christi   Thursday 10 days after Pentecost Sunday
- ♦ St Peter and St Paul   June 29

Note: If a Feast Day falls on a Saturday or Monday it transfers to the Sunday.

Ash Wednesday is not a holy day of obligation.

The Liturgical Year graphically

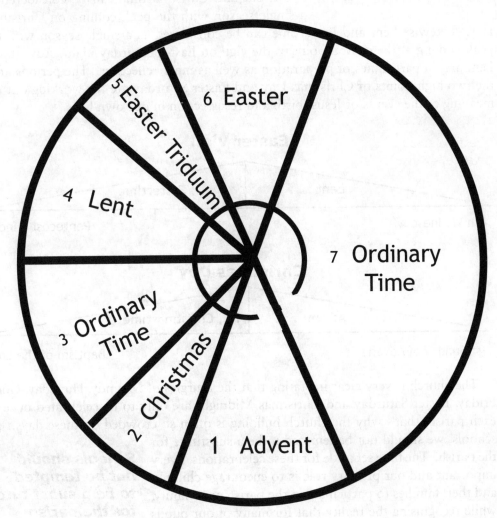

The school year

Our present three-term school year follows the church's cycle in that two of our long holidays coincide with the celebration of Christmas Day and Easter Sunday.

But this creates a dilemma. How do we celebrate these feasts in school? How, for instance, can we celebrate Advent as a four week season while we are preparing Christmas plays and rehearsing carols? How can we celebrate the Triduum liturgies with the commemoration of Christ's death and resurrection when we are on holiday over the Easter weekend?

Advent and Christmastime can be considered as a single season with the peak coming on Christmas Day. Likewise Lent and Eastertime can be considered as a single season with the peak coming at the central point of the vigil on Easter Saturday night. Advent and Lent are, in part, times of preparation as well as inner reflection. The periods after the two high points of Christmas Day and Easter Saturday are for working out the meaning of the events of Jesus' birth and resurrection in our own lives.

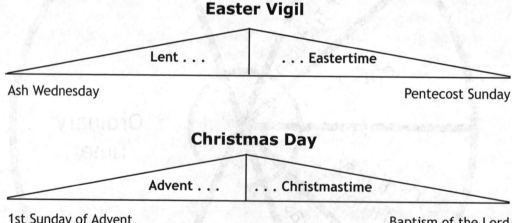

The church is very clear in stating that the liturgies of Maundy Thursday, Good Friday, Easter Saturday and Christmas Midnight are only to be celebrated once in each parish; that's why the church building is often so crowded on these days. As schools, we should not be tempted to be a substitute for the parish. The time set aside for these celebrations is very important and our primary role is to encourage children and their families to participate in the parish community, while recognising the reality that for many of our pupils school is their faith base.

Schools should not be tempted to be a substitute for the parish

We can help by preparing the children to understand these liturgies and by reflecting on them in our school celebrations afterwards but we cannot do them in school, much though we would perhaps want to. It may be felt that some children who are not active members of a parish will 'miss out' but our hope is that we are preparing them to have full, active participation as members of a parish in the future.

Be bold - don't anticipate Christmas or Easter

It is a bold move for any school to begin to celebrate Advent for the full four weeks and not to anticipate Christmas but celebrate it when the school returns in January. Celebrating one or two Advent liturgies will not make up for the richness offered in that whole season.

With Lent, we seem more at ease with celebrating the season for its full six weeks although we may be tempted to round off the spring term by celebrating an Easter liturgy of the resurrection. But don't. Wait until the beginning of the summer term when you will have fifty days to celebrate!

However, a word of warning. If we want to change our current practice know that it cannot be fixed in an instant. It will probably take many years to pull the liturgical seasons back into their proper place in the school's calendar. People of other faiths living in this country know what it is to go against the tide of the civic year and their religious celebrations are often at odds with the cultural norms of shopping sales and holidays.

This isn't to say we can't tell the stories of Christmas and Easter in plays and prayerful celebrations before the proper season begins, but we really should not be proclaiming the scriptures of those days in a liturgy until the appointed times. Changing Palm Sunday to 'Palm Monday' denies everyone their connection to the world church and is making the school into an alternative parish.

In my own school, we currently have this overlap of the seasons. On the first Monday of Advent we celebrate a whole school liturgy with the blessing of the Advent wreath, but the next week we see the hall decorated with Christmas stars and display boards telling the nativity story! We will need to go through a process of reflection and planning for change over a number of years in order to begin to celebrate Advent more fully and put the Christmas season in its correct place ie from Christmas Day until January 11, not from mid-November to Boxing Day. To begin with it may feel odd to do so but I believe we are missing the whole richness of Advent and need to reclaim the strengths that come from that period of darkness, anticipation and preparation.

How do school liturgies relate to the Sunday?

Sunday and School

Sunday is 'the day of the Lord' and the principal day in each week when the Christian community comes together for Eucharist. Schools are not expected to supply a replacement for the Sunday Mass that many of the children may not have been able to participate in. What we can consider doing is celebrating a short Liturgy of the Word on the Monday using the Gospel reading from the day before. Here we are not 're-celebrating' the Sunday event but reflecting upon the scripture together and seeing how it can affect our lives together in the coming week, listening to how the word can echo and resonate for us as individuals and as a school community. This is known as 'mystagogy' – leading the newly initiated/baptised person into greater reflection on the mysteries already celebrated.

Each Monday we have an assembly with the whole school (nursery to year 6 plus all the staff) to celebrate the scripture of the previous day.

Every class brings its prayer candle which is lit from the large central candle on a low table in front of the children. We begin with a greeting and the sign of the cross followed by a proclamation of the Gospel, read by the head teacher from a wooden lectern covered in a cloth in the colour of the liturgical season. Occasionally we choose the first reading or psalm instead. There is a time of quiet reflection followed by a brief exploration of the Gospel, led by a member of staff, of what the text may mean to us today in our home lives, in our school lives and in relation to the world. We end with a short communal prayer, dismissal and song.

To mark the end of the liturgical assembly and the beginning of our 'business' assembly that follows immediately, the head teacher invites a child to snuff out all the candles. For some reason all the children then burst into applause, a practice we have decided to keep as it was the children's initial enthusiastic response to the action and would take a lot of persuasion to change! The little ones take great pleasure in waving their hands gently through the wafting smoke...

I can never think of a theme for my assembly

Thinking of a theme

Many assembly books written for schools offer themes or topics to be celebrated throughout the year – one on 'courage', one on 'friends', one on 'special gifts' and so on. Often a school has established a schedule for celebrating Mass or a special liturgy once a week or once a fortnight and a theme is searched for on each occasion.

The church's year does not follow a weekly pattern like the school curriculum term. What it does have are enough seasons and feasts to celebrate without ever having to look around for another theme. Remember that the central motif that runs through every liturgy is the Paschal Mystery, that is the mystery of Christ's suffering, death, resurrection and ascension into glory. The seasons of the year and special days allow us to look at this same reality each time, but from different viewpoints and with different emphases on particular aspects.

By looking to the liturgical calendar for scripture texts and prayers we will find every opportunity we need in the year to celebrate the fullness of our lives as Christians. Go back to this basic and rich resource. Look again at what the church is giving us for each day and season.

The liturgies outlined later in this book follow the church's cycle rather than the many invented themes that can muddy the clear waters of what already exists to nourish and refresh us. Schools using the HIA programme will notice that the three set topics for each term follow the liturgical year. The celebrations planned for the 'Reflect' and 'Respond' times could take the form of a class or whole school liturgy.

Plan ahead

When is the schedule for your school's year of celebrations drawn up? Consider mapping out the whole year from September to July so that you can allow for preparation and reflection time, a sharing of the responsibility in leadership and the pre-eminence of the school's liturgical life over other events. For instance, Lent is not the time for concerts and parties – save those for the Easter season.

Apart from the holy days of obligation, when Mass is usually part of the school day, look to the liturgical year to find the feasts and seasons that could be celebrated in a well planned liturgy of the word style assembly.

The school's patronal feast or anniversary of foundation may be added to your diary as well as the two Fast Days appointed by CAFOD (the Catholic Agency for Overseas Development) and ecumenical events such as the week of prayer for Christian unity. This would give between fifteen and twenty non-eucharistic liturgies in the whole school year which is certainly manageable, especially if the task of planning, preparing and leading is shared between staff and classes.

Month:				Year:		
Sunday	Monday	Tuesday	Wednesday	Thursday	Friday	Saturday

11 SAMPLE LITURGIES

1. Template for a Liturgy of the Word

WE GATHER TOGETHER

Opening responses

Leader: We come together to pray –
All: **in the name of the Father,
and of the Son,
and of the holy Spirit.**
Amen.
Leader: O God open our lips
All: **And we shall praise your name**

Opening words *(...brief introduction/context/season...)*

Song

Opening Prayer *(...use from missal for season or compose your own...)*

Leader: O God...
You... Your...
Give us/
guide us/
watch over us/
help us/
make us/
lead us/
May we...
We ask this through Jesus Christ our Lord
All: Amen.

WE PROCLAIM THE WORD OF GOD

Invitation

Reader: Let us listen to this reading from the Bible

For readings other than the Gospel

Reader: A reading from ...

After the reading

Reader: This is the word of the Lord
All: **Thanks be to God**

For Gospel readings

Reader: A reading from the Gospel of Saint...
All: **Glory to you, O Lord**

After the Gospel reading

Reader: This is the Gospel of the Lord
All: **Praise to you, Lord Jesus Christ**

WE RESPOND IN PRAYER AND ACTION

RITUAL ACTION

(...different in each liturgy...)

INTERCESSORY PRAYER

Introduction

Leader: A   We know that God loves us,
                   so let us pray for ourselves and for others.

or   B   We are God's family, filled with the Holy Spirit,
                   together let us pray.

or   C   Jesus has told us to ask God for what we need,
                   so as God's children we pray.

Intentions

Intercessor: We pray for...
              the church/ the world/ those in need/ local
                   community/ sick/ deceased
              May they/it...

Reader: Lord, in your mercy
All: **Hear our prayer**

or   We pray to the Lord
              Lord, hear our prayer

or   We pray to Christ the Lord
              Christ, hear us.

Concluding Prayer

Leader: A   Loving God,
We ask you to listen to these prayers
Which we bring to you today
In the name of Jesus the Lord.

All: **Amen.**

or   B   Father,
May your love be with us always
And bring peace and joy to our families.
We ask this through Jesus Christ our Lord.

All: **Amen.**

or   C   God of tender love
You always hear our prayers
We ask you to grant us what we need
Through Jesus Christ our Lord.

All: **Amen.**

WE LEAVE

Blessing

Leader: May God, who (...*interject seasonal phrase* ...) bless us
All: **In the name of the Father
and of the Son
and of the Holy Spirit.
Amen.**

Dismissal

Leader: Our celebration/assembly/time of prayer has ended.
      Let us go in the peace of Christ
All: **Thanks be to God**

Song

ACKNOWLEDGMENT. In the following pages, Scripture readings and prayers marked 'Sunday' are reprinted from The SUNDAY Liturgy of the Word Series with the permission of the publisher and copyright holders: Forum Katecheticum and Treehaus Communications, Inc., P.O. Box 249, Loveland, Ohio 45140 USA, (http://www.treehaus1.com/). All rights are reserved. Distributed in the United Kingdom by Viewpoint Resources Direct, 21 Point Hill, Greenwich LONDON SE10 8QW England.

2 Liturgy for the Beginning of Advent

WE GATHER TOGETHER

Opening responses

Leader: We come together to pray -
All: **in the name of the Father,
and of the Son,
and of the Holy Spirit.
Amen.**

Leader: O God, open our lips.
All: **and we shall praise your name.**

Song

Opening words....

*Advent is the beginning of the Church year..., doesn't start in January...,
notice we are using the colour purple ...., look out for change of colour on
Sunday.., four weeks to this season - a count down to Christmas which will
then last for twelve days...*

Opening Prayer

God, you love us so much
you want to be among us.
Make us ready to welcome you
by following your ways
and living at peace with one another.
We ask you to do this through Christ, our Lord.
Amen.

WE PROCLAIM THE WORD OF GOD

Leader: A reading from the Gospel of Matthew
                    (Matthew 24:42-44)

All: **Glory to you. Lord.**

Jesus said to his disciples,
'Stay awake! Always be ready! You do not know when your Lord is coming.
You know that if the owners of a house knew at what time of night a thief
was coming, they would stay awake and would not allow the thief to break
into their house. Well, in the same way, you must always be ready because
you do not know the time when the Lord is coming.'

Leader: This is the Gospel of the Lord.
All: **Praise to you, Lord Jesus Christ.**

from Sunday: see p.89

RITUAL ACTION

Briefly explain the significance of the undecorated Advent wreath to the children. A circle shape to show the everlasting love of God..., four candles to mark the four Sundays of Advent..., one candle to mark the season of Christmas, which lasts for twelve days..., evergreen leaves to symbolise the eternal nature of God.

In advance, each group/class in the school has been given a ribbon (about 30cm long, red and/or purple). As an Advent song is sung, a representative from each group comes forward to tie a ribbon onto the wreath. Everyone in the celebration watches to see where 'their' ribbon is tied.

Bless the wreath - all extend hands over the wreath. Perhaps have someone hold it high. Light the first purple candle.

Blessing for the Advent Wreath

> O God, you created the whole universe.
> We ask you to bless this Advent wreath
> which we have created together.
> May the light of the candles
> be sign of Christ's love and warmth.
> May we bring light and warmth
> into the darkness of other people's lives this Advent.
> We ask this through Jesus Christ, our Lord.
> **Amen.**

PRAYER

Leader: We know that God loves us,
so let us pray for ourselves and for others.

Reader: We pray for Christian people all over the world.
May we all get ready for Christmas in a joyful way.
Lord, in your mercy.

All: **Hear our prayer.**

Reader: We pray for leaders in our school and in our town.
May they make fair and wise decisions.
Lord, in your mercy.

All: **Hear our prayer.**

Reader: We pray for ourselves.
May we bring fairness and peace into our school
and homes this Advent.
Lord, in your mercy.

All: **Hear our prayer.**

Reader: We pray for people who do not have the things
they need to live.
May they have food, warmth and love.
Lord, in your mercy.
All: **Hear our prayer.**

Closing Prayer

God, you are the light
that shines in the darkness,
Just as this candle shines.
Help us to be ready
to welcome you into our lives
by shining our light of joy
into all we do and say.
We ask this through Jesus Christ our Lord.
Amen.

WE LEAVE

Blessing

Leader: In this season of Advent, may God bless us
All: **in the name of the Father,**
and of the Son,
and of the Holy Spirit.
Amen.

Dismissal

Leader: Our assembly is ended.
Let us go in the peace of Christ.
All: **Thanks be to God.**

Song

Suggested songs:
- 0 come, o come, Emmanuel
- Stay awake, be ready - Laudate
- Winter time. Advent time - Rejoice Book 2
- Christmas is coming, the Church is glad to sing - Laudate
- Circle Song (Bernadette Farrell) - Share the Light

3 Liturgy for the Beginning of Lent

WE GATHER TOGETHER

Opening responses

Leader: We come together to pray -

All: **in the name of the Father,
and of the Son,
and of the holy Spirit.
Amen.**

Leader: O God open our lips

All: **and we shall praise your name.**

Opening words

This week is the first week in the season called Lent. There will be six weeks in Lent before Easter time. In these six weeks we are asked to pray, to give to charities and to fast from some of the rich things we have.

Song

Opening Prayer

Leader: God our protector,
you wanted Jesus to be one with us.
We are sometimes tempted to be greedy,
to control other people's lives,
and to forget that all good things come from you.
Hold us in your care
and never let us forsake you.
We ask you this through Christ our Lord.

All: **Amen.**

from Sunday: see p.89

WE PROCLAIM THE WORD OF GOD

Invitation

Reader: Let us listen to this reading from the Bible.

[For readings other than the Gospel]

Reader: A reading from ...

Reader: This is the word of the Lord.

All: **Thanks be to God.**

[For Gospel reading]

Reader: A reading from the Gospel of Saint Luke   *(Luke 4:1-13)*

All: **Glory to you, O Lord.**

After Jesus was baptized in the Jordan River,
the Spirit led him into the desert for forty days,
and the devil tried to tempt him.
For all those days, Jesus did not eat any foot,
and he was hungry.
So, the devil said to Jesus:
   'If you are the Son of God, tell this stone to become bread.'
But Jesus said to the devil:
   'It is written in the books of Moses,
   "People do not live just by eating food."'
Then the devil took Jesus up and showed him
all the kingdoms of the world, and said:
   'I will give you all the power and glory of these kingdoms if you will worship
   me.'
But Jesus said,
   'It is written in the books of Moses,
   "You must worship God, and only God!"'
Then the devil took Jesus to the very top of the temple in Jerusalem, and said to him:
   'If you are the Son of God, jump down from here,
   because it is written in the book of Psalms,
   "God will tell the angels to take care of you,
   and they will catch you
   so that you will not hurt your foot on a rock."'
But Jesus said,
   'It is also written,
   "You shall not test your God."'
After these temptations, the devil left Jesus and waited for another time to come
again.

     Reader: This is the Gospel of the Lord.
     All: **Praise to you, Lord Jesus Christ.**

from Sunday: see p.89

WE RESPOND IN PRAYER AND ACTION

RITUAL ACTION

Copy out each letter of the word ALLELUIA (it means 'Praise the Lord') onto a piece of A4 card. Muddle up the order of the letters. Show the assembled children the cards and ask them what they think the letters spell. Have a group of the younger children come out to hold the letters and an older child to rearrange the children with the cards to spell out ALLELUIA correctly. It may take a few attempts! Once the word is clearly visible to everyone, sing a familiar Alleluia song a number of times, reducing the volume on each singing so that eventually the song dies out. Explain to the children that this word is now no longer sung until Easter. We are starting a time of fasting, fasting from the joyous words of Easter as well as from rich foods and activities. Collect in the cards and tie them up with a beautiful ribbon. Invite one child to hide the package somewhere in the hall, somewhere that it can rest for the next six weeks and not be disturbed.

INTERCESSORY PRAYER
Introduction

Leader:	Jesus has told us to ask God for what we need, so as God's children we pray.

Intentions

Intercessor:	We pray for... *the church/ the world/ those in need/ local community/ sick/* *deceased* May they/it...
Reader:	Lord, in your mercy
All:	**Hear our prayer.**

Concluding Prayer

Leader:	God of tender love You always hear our prayers We ask you to grant us what we need Through Jesus Christ our Lord.
All:	**Amen.**

WE LEAVE
Blessing

Leader:	May God, who calls us and helps us to change our lives, bless us
All:	**in the name of the Father** **and of the Son** **and of the Holy Spirit.** **Amen.**

Dismissal

Leader:	Our liturgy is ended. Let us go in the peace of Christ
All:	**Thanks be to God.**

Song

> **Suggested songs:**
> - Children of God (Calling the Children)
> - Don't be afraid (Come, all you people)
> - Forty days and forty nights (Laudate)
> - Here I am, Lord (Laudate)
> - Oh Lord, hear my prayer (Taizé) - Laudate
> - There is someone (Bernadette Farrell) - Share the Light
> - The Servant Song - Laudate

4 Liturgy for the Beginning of Eastertide

WE GATHER TOGETHER

Opening Responses

Leader: We come together to pray -
All: **in the name of the Father,**
        and of the Son,
        and of the Holy Spirit.
        Amen.

Leader: O God, open our lips.
All: **and we shall praise your name.**

Opening words....

We have come together today to start a new term together. In the holiday the church celebrated the great feast of Easter. Easter time lasts for 50 days. The colours of the cloths have now changed to white and gold. All around us there are signs of new life. We are celebrating because we believe that Jesus is risen and is alive now.

Song

Opening Prayer

Leader: God of everything that lives,
        we are happy today
        because Jesus was dead and now he is alive,
        and through our baptism
        you give us a share in his life.
        By what we do and say,
        make us true sisters and brothers of Jesus
        and of each other,
        and so live together forever and ever.
        We ask this through Jesus Christ our Lord
All: **Amen.**

WE PROCLAIM THE WORD OF GOD

Reader: Listen to this reading from the Bible. Try to understand what the
            words mean to you and your life.
            A reading from the Gospel of Matthew   *(Matthew 28:1-10)*

All: **Glory to you, O Lord.**

On the first day of the week, very early in the morning, Mary Magdalene
and another woman named Mary went to the tomb where Jesus was buried.
 Suddenly, there was a big earthquake,
and an angel of God came down from heaven.
The angel rolled the stone away from in front of the tomb and sat on it.
The angel was wearing bright white clothes that were shining like lightning.
The soldiers who were guarding the tomb were very frightened,
and they fell down like they were dead!
Then the angel said to the women,
> 'Don't be afraid. I know you are looking for Jesus who was crucified. But
> he isn't here. He has been raised from the dead, just as he said he would.
> Come and see the place where his body was laid. Now, hurry and tell his
> disciples about this. Say to them,
> "Jesus has risen from the dead. He is going to Galilee where you will see
> him."'

So the women hurried away.
They were filled with joy, but they were also a little afraid.
Suddenly, Jesus was standing right in front of them.
He said, 'Peace!'
The women fell down and hugged his feet
and worshipped him.
Then Jesus said, 'Don't be afraid.
  Go and tell my disciples
  that they must go to Galilee where they will see me.'
This is the gospel of the Lord

All: **Praise to you, Lord Jesus Christ.**   from Sunday: see p.89

WE RESPOND IN PRAYER AND ACTION

RITUAL ACTION

At the beginning of Lent, you buried the letters of the word ALLELUIA. Now
is the time to rediscover the word and display it for all to see.

*Ask the children to recall what was hidden all those weeks ago(p.95). What did we
hide? Who chose the special hiding place? Can you remember where he/she hid
it? Invite a child to come and look for the hidden tin (make sure it hasn't been
moved in the holiday spring clean!). Untie the bow and bring out the eight letters.
As you did in the Lent assembly, invite eight children to hold up the letters in a
muddled order and then ask another child to reorder the letters so that they form*

A-L-L-E-L-U-I-A. Now is the time to sing your school Alleluia song, starting softly and gradually getting louder. The letters can then form part of an Easter display in the assembly hall.

INTERCESSORY PRAYER

Introduction

Leader: We are God's family.
Filled with the Holy Spirit,
together let us pray.

Intentions

Intercessor: We pray for...
the church/ the world/
those in need/ local community/
sick/ deceased
May they/it...

Reader: We pray to Christ the Lord
All: **Christ hear us**

Concluding Prayer

Leader: Risen Lord,
may your love be with us always
and bring peace and joy to our families.
We ask this through Jesus Christ our Lord.
All: **Amen.**

WE LEAVE

Blessing

Leader: May God, who made us his children, bless us
All: **in the name of the Father
and of the Son
and of the Holy Spirit.
Amen.**

Dismissal

Leader: Our assembly has ended.
Let us go in the peace of Christ
All: **Thanks be to God.**

Song

Suggested songs:
• Alleluia, give thanks - Laudate
• Halle, halle - Laudate
• Now the green blade riseth - Laudate
• Share the light of Jesus - Share the Light
• Shine, Jesus, shine - Laudate
• Uyai Mose - Come, all you people
• We are the Church - Calling the Children

5 A Liturgy for Remembrance

WE GATHER

Opening Responses

Leader: We come together to pray -
All: **in the name of the Father,**
                 and of the Son,
                 and of the Holy Spirit. Amen.

Leader: O God, open our lips.
All: **and we shall praise your name.**

Opening words....

We have come together as a school to remember the people we know who have died. Some will have been part of our family, some may have been our friends. As Christians, we believe that life carries on after death but in a new way. Our bodies are not needed any more but our souls or spirits keep on living.

Song

Opening Prayer

Leader: God, you are with us always.
               You love us and care for us.
               Watch over us today as we remember our family and friends
                     who have died.
               May we remember with happiness the love and care they showed
for us.
               We ask this through Jesus Christ our Lord
All: **Amen.**

WE PROCLAIM THE WORD OF GOD

Reader: Listen to this reading from the Bible.

A reading from the first letter of Paul to the Thessalonians   *1 Thess 4:13-18*

My friends, we want you to understand how it will be
for those followers who have already died.
Then you won't grieve over them
           and be like people who don't have any hope.
Encourage each other with these words.
This is the word of the Lord
Thanks be to God.

WE RESPOND IN PRAYER AND ACTION

RITUAL ACTION

About a week before this act of worship, each group in the school should be given a piece of red card/paper with 'We Remember' printed at the top. Some time can be taken in the class to help the children reflect on the names they might record on the class list. Many will have to ask at home for the names of grandparents or other relatives. Show sensitivity towards those who have lost a close family member such as a parent or sibling. I have found that children find this opportunity to talk about their lives very strengthening and they are usually very open in talking about a deceased relative. For some children a pet is the only 'person' they have lost. Adult groups (admin/cleaning staff and parents) should also be invited to add names.

During the assembly, a representative from each group (child and adult) stands in their place, holds up their card and announces its presence with words such as:

'These are the names that Miss Fletcher's class would like to remember'
or
'The office staff would like to remember these people who have died.'

The representative then comes forward to pin the card to the board or to place it in a book of remembrance. After two or three representatives have come forward, sing verse one of 'Abide with me.'
When all the cards have been brought forward, take a minute to be silent.

'We close our eyes now and try to keep our bodies and our minds very relaxed and still. Use this time of silence to remember the people whose names you had written on the card.'

PRAYER

(To be learned in the week leading up to the assembly and have up on OHP. Also possible to do as two prayers - one with feminine pronouns, one with masculine)

We say together a special prayer of the church for those who have died:
Eternal rest grant unto them, O Lord,
and let perpetual light shine upon them.
May they rest in peace. Amen.

WE LEAVE

Blessing

Leader: May God, who gives comfort to all who are sad, bless us
All: **In the name of the Father**
            and of the Son
            and of the Holy Spirit. Amen.

Dismissal

Leader: Our assembly has ended.
           Let us go in the peace of Christ
All: **Thanks be to God.**

Song

> **Suggested songs:**
> • Abide with me *and*
> Song of Farewell (chorus) - Laudate
> • I am special - Share the Light
> • Behold the Lamb of God *and*
> • Don't be afraid - Come, all you people

12 Endings

ONE DANGER OF SITTING AT A COMPUTER FOR WEEKS ON END is that the ideals take prominence over reality. Many times when I have emerged to life beyond this small room and desk, I have been knocked forcibly from my lofty isolation back to life on earth by witnessing a fight on the bus, seeing a yellow police incident sign erected, despairing over yet another broken fence, reading an appeal letter from Amnesty about rape in Rwanda, hearing a radio news flash of terrorist violence. And I return to the computer thinking 'Why am I bothering to write about liturgy?'

I am bothering because liturgy speaks to all of life including the violent, the mundane, the emotional, the irritating, the shocking. It is because of doing liturgy, in school, in church, with friends, that I can face dealing with the everyday parts of life.

You will know that teaching is extremely hard work. It can be tiring, stressful and all-consuming – certainly not a profession for the weak! So, doesn't all that is described in these chapters just add more to the pile of tasks? Yes... but very soon it will feed you too in order that you can more easily do all the other things you are called to do.

In writing I have reflected so often on practice at my own school and have thought of the many things we could change in the future (most are simplifications rather than complications). But not everything can or even ought to be changed at once. Other staff must be on board to do this gradually – the process of discussion and change can be life-giving in itself.

At the end of the spring term, we have an 'Easter Reflection' when the whole school gathers one afternoon at the parish hall.

Children sit in class groups in wedges around a central focus and parents sit around the outer circle. It is the only time in the year when everyone comes together. In the middle of the floor is an arrangement of lenten coloured cloths, a large wooden cross and the lectionary. Each member of staff reads a small section of the Passion narrative, starting at the entry of Jesus into Jerusalem and ending with the two Marys at the empty tomb. A child carries the cross and lectionary from adult to adult and each class stands in turn to mime their part of the story. Between each reading, and sometimes underneath the reading, we sing or hum a song.

This year, for the first time, we added dance to some of the songs and ended with a blessing and quiet music instead of the more usual loud Gospel song. We left the hall gently singing a song from South Africa called 'Bambelela' – which means 'keep holding on.'

This is the eighth year we have celebrated in this way, each time moving to a more simple and prayerful structure. In the succeeding days staff talked often about the experience and began to reflect on whether we could change what we do in the other seasons to be more like this Easter Reflection. It is likely that we will plan next year to go to the parish hall four times – Advent, post Christmas holiday, Lent and Easter – to celebrate the events of each season as a whole school rather than having our current run of nativity plays and concerts.

Changes can only be taken on fully if the energy for them has emerged from those who will work with them. They cannot be imposed.

At our school, when days feel long and the tasks to be achieved overwhelming, the head teacher says simply: 'The only way to eat an elephant is in little pieces.' Now, we don't always want to eat the elephant but the metaphor is wonderful for reminding us that big changes can only happen slowly.

Lavina Byrne, the religious writer and broadcaster, calls her autobiography *The Journey Is My Home*. Begin the journey soon but do not expect to ever arrive. You will be granted resting places along the way, moments when you will look around in awe and say, as God did at creation 'It is good.' Then you must walk on again, together.

I encourage you to reflect on and evaluate what you are doing *well* at the moment. Highlight the good things that you want to keep then take a long and wide view of how you want to change just as you would for a school development plan.

Don't try to do everything at once but chose one or two fundamental changes that could have a huge effect. Always try to keep colleagues, including the head teacher and parish priest, with you even if you are wanting to go at a faster pace. You may find that your own creative ideas are developing all the time, but be aware that if you introduce a new practice it must be given time for much repetition. Once established well it need not be changed each year.

reflect on what you are doing well at the moment

This ending chapter was written over the Easter holidays, a time when thoughts of death and resurrection are close at hand. A friend of mine belongs to a drama performance group called 'Ups and Downs', named so because the members are all young people with Downs syndrome. I have learned from my time with this young woman and her family that life for her is marked by sudden ups and downs of emotion. No one living their lives to the full has a smooth journey; in the course of one day we may experience moments of both death and resurrection. The times of 'death' may feel overwhelming at the time but if only we look back and remember past experiences of resurrection we would have more courage to enter the darker places.

I hope the ideas in this book have not brought you to a place of discouragement about your own situation. Instead, I hope that they inspire you to have that courage to enter a long, gradual process of change and growth for your whole school community.

If you want to walk fast, walk alone. But if you want to go far, walk together with others.
African Proverb

Resources

Church Documents

Directory for Masses with Children: Supplement to the General Instruction of the Roman Missal, 1973.

Liturgy of the Word with Children: Guidelines. Bishops' Conference of England and Wales, 1996

Books

Children in the Assembly of the Church: Eleanor Bernstein CSJ and John Brooks-Leonard, editors. Liturgy Training Publications (LTP) 1992.

The Welcome Table - Planning Masses with Children: Elizabeth McMahon Jeep et al. LTP 1982

Preparing Liturgy for Children and Children for Liturgy (formerly *Leader's Manual for Hymnal for Catholic Students*). Gabe Huck et al. LTP/GIA Publications 1989

School Year Church Year- Customs and Decorations for the Classroom: Peter Mazar. LTP 2001

All the above available from Decani Music, Oak House, 70 High Street, Brandon IP27 OAU 0845 456 8392

A Child Shall Lead Them - A guide to celebrating the Word with children. Gerard A. Pottebaum and others. Treehaus Communications, Inc.

Sunday - Book of Readings Years A, B and C (Treehaus.)
Sunday - Leader's Guidebook Years A, B and C (Treehaus.)

To Walk With A Child - How to prepare a homily for children: Gerard A. Pottebaum. (Treehaus.)

Treehaus books available from Viewpoint Resources Direct, 21 Point Hill, London SE10 8QW, 020 8692 1138 www.viewpoint24.com

Music

Something Fischy; Build UP; These Are Our Emotions: Music and resource books plus cds with backing tracks. Songs, without specific religious language, which deal with issues of self-esteem, family life, bullying, friendship and emotions.

Available from: Fischy Music, 45 Queensferry Street Lane, Edinburgh EH2 4PF. 0131 225 3344, www.fischy.com

Share The Light book/CD/CD-rom: Songs that enable the young to pray from the heart. (CD-rom demonstrates British Sign Language for lyrics.) Bernadette Farrell, OCP Publications

Calling the Children - book/CD: Songs specifically written for primary children. Christopher Walker, OCP Publications.

Come All You People book/CD - short chants and responses: Wild Goose Publications

Sent By The Lord - book/CD - songs from the world church: Wild Goose Publications

Laudate - hymn book with traditional and contemporary songs and chants: Decani, 1999

Available from Decani (above)

Useful Addresses

CAFOD Catholic Agency For Overseas Development
Romero Close, London SW9 9TY
020 7733 7900
www.cafod.org.uk

Christian Aid
35 Lower Marsh, London SE1 7RL
020 7620 4444
www.christian-aid.org.uk

Catholic Education Service
39 Eccleston Square, London SW1V 1BX
020 7901 4880
www.cesew.org.uk

Bishops' Conference of England and Wales
The Liturgy Office,
39 Eccleston Square
London SW1V IPL
www.catholicchurch.org.uk